Sales God: Rise to the Top and Rule the Sales World

by Gnaneshwar

Copyright Page

Sales God: Rise to the Top and Rule the Sales World
Copyright © 2024 by Gnaneshwar

All rights reserved. No part of this publication may be reproduced, distributed, or transmitted in any form or by any means, including photocopying, recording, or other electronic or mechanical methods, without the prior written permission of the publisher, except in the case of brief quotations embodied in critical reviews and certain other noncommercial uses permitted by copyright law.

Inspired by Personal Experiences and Self-Learning:
This ebook is a reflection of my personal journey in sales, business, and personal development, combining years of experience and self-education. Many of the insights and strategies within these pages have been cultivated from real-life applications, personal successes, and lessons learned through both failure and triumph.

Inspiration from Great Books:
Additionally, this book draws upon the wisdom and teachings from some of the most influential and renowned books on sales and business available in the market. These works have been a valuable source of inspiration, and their teachings have been expanded upon and enriched with my own experiences and unique perspectives to provide readers with enhanced and actionable insights.

Disclaimer: The information provided in this book is for general informational purposes only. The author is not a licensed financial advisor, and the content should not be construed as financial, legal, or other professional advice.

Cover design by Karthik.S

First edition: September, 2024

Dedication

To the relentless hustlers, dreamers, and doers who wake up every day ready to rule their world.

Introduction

Welcome to "Sales God: Rise to the Top and Rule the Sales World." If you're reading this, you're ready to master the world of sales and rise to the top of your game. This isn't just another sales book filled with vague advice. This is your road map to becoming a powerhouse in the sales world.

In this book, I'll show you how to grab attention, build trust, master the art of persuasion, and close deals like never before. Whether you're a sales veteran or just starting out, the principles here will guide you on your journey to becoming the ultimate sales god.

Sales isn't just about selling a product—it's about dominating your market, understanding human psychology, and mastering the art of influence. Throughout this book, I'll teach you the tools, strategies, and mindset shifts needed to close deals with confidence and build lasting relationships that translate into long-term success.

Let's get started.

INDEX

1. Be Attention Grabber: Make Them Look, Make Them Buy
2. Influence to Income: Turn Attention into Profit
3. The Power of First Impressions
4. Sell the Story, Not the Product
5. Build Trust, Build Loyalty, Generate Sales
6. Create Urgency: Make Them Buy Now
7. Turn On Customer 'Oh No No' into 'Oh Yes Yes'
8. Sell the Experience, Close the Deal: Master Emotional Selling
9. Loyalty Goldmine: Keep Them Coming Back
10. Upsell Like a Boss: Boost Sales
11. Networking: The Hidden Key to Sales Success
12. Close with Confidence: Seal the Deal
13. Emotional Intelligence in Sales: Connecting on a Deeper Level
14. Cash Control: Master Your Money and Grow Your Wealth
15. Scaling Your Business: Grow Big, Scale Fast
16. Nail the Close: Finish Strong and Seal the Deal
17. Managing Stress in Sales: Strategies for Sustaining Success
18. Handling Difficult Customers

19. The Role of Creativity in Sales
20. Why Should the Customer Buy?
21. Turn Customers into Your Sales Team
22. Adapting to Change: Staying Agile in Sales
23. The Psychology of Money: Changing Your Mindset
24. Cash Flow Power: Control the Money, Control the Game
25. Brand Like a Boss: Rule Your Market
26. Bank on Social Proof: Transform Testimonials into Cash
27. Road Map to Wealth: Financial Planning for Entrepreneurs
28. The Power of Consistency: Building Habits for Long-Term Success
29. The Power of Mindset: Cultivating a Winning Mentality
30. Investing in Yourself: The Best Investment You'll Ever Make
31. Passive Income Strategies: Building Wealth While You Sleep
32. Mindset Shifts for Financial Success
33. Customers Are So Dumb (But That's Your Opportunity)

34. Understanding Customer Behavior: The Key to Tailored Sales Strategies
35. Value Your Worth: Get What You Deserve
36. Give More Than You Charge: The Secret to Lasting Success
37. Master the Art of Negotiation: Closing Deals with Confidence
38. The 80/20 Rule: How It Works in Sales and Business
39. Give It Free, Charge Later
40. Do It Now or Regret Later
41. Content is King: Make Your Mark in the Digital World
42. Don't Consume, Just Sell
43. Kill Procrastination — Or It Will Kill You
44. Don't Allow Money to Ruin Your Relations

Chapter 1:
Be Attention Grabber: Make Them Look, Make Them Buy

In today's fast-paced world, attention isn't just a commodity—it's the currency of success. The marketplace is a battleground where businesses fight for the same prize: the customer's focus. But here's the hard truth: If you're not grabbing attention, you're invisible. And in this game, invisibility equals failure.

Why Attention Equals Money

Let's not sugarcoat it—without attention, you're dead in the water. Think about it: why do social media influencers post those outrageous videos, or why do brands launch campaigns that push the envelope? It's simple—they understand that attention leads to money. The more eyeballs you have on you, the more potential customers you have, and the more money you can make.

Take the classic example of the "fake drama" strategy used by countless celebrities. They create buzz with controversial statements or actions, not because they care about the drama itself, but because they know it keeps them in the public eye. More views, more engagement, more sales.

Strategies to Command Attention

So, how do you make sure you're the one everyone's talking about? Here's how:

1. **Create a Spectacle:**
   - **Go Big or Go Home:** Sometimes, subtlety just doesn't cut it. Think about the last marketing campaign that really caught your eye. Chances are, it wasn't something low-key. It was bold, loud, and impossible to ignore. Whether it's an outrageous stunt, a viral video, or a daring social media campaign, the goal is to stop people in their tracks.
   - **Be Unexpected:** Do something that people don't see coming. When Netflix released the movie "The Cloverfield Paradox" without any prior announcement during the Super Bowl, it shocked audiences and made headlines instantly. It was unexpected, and it got people talking.

2. **Leverage Controversy:**
   - **Controlled Chaos:** Controversy can be a double-edged sword, but when used correctly, it can propel your brand into the spotlight. Look at brands like Ben & Jerry's—they aren't afraid to take a stand on social issues, and while it may alienate some, it solidifies their brand identity and attracts a loyal following.
   - **The Kanye Effect:** Kanye West is a master at staying relevant through controversy. Whether it's interrupting award shows or making bold statements, he knows that controversy keeps him in the headlines. While it's risky, it's a proven strategy for those who aren't afraid to push boundaries.

3. **Tell a Story That Sticks:**
   - **Emotion Over Information:** People don't remember data—they remember stories that made them feel something. Share the journey of your brand, the hurdles you've overcome, or the mission that drives you. For example, TOMS Shoes didn't just sell shoes; they sold the story of giving a pair to someone in need for every pair purchased.

That story was powerful, and it resonated deeply with customers.
- **Use Visual Storytelling**: In the age of Instagram and TikTok, visuals are king. Use photos, videos, and infographics to tell your story in a way that's visually engaging. A well-crafted video can convey more emotion and information in 60 seconds than a page of text ever could.

Turning Attention into Profit

Getting attention is only the first step. You need to turn those eyeballs into action. Here's how to convert attention into sales:

1. Clear Call to Action:

- **Direct and Simple:** Don't make people guess what you want them to do. Whether it's "Buy Now," "Sign Up," or "Learn More," your call to action (CTA) should be direct and easy to follow. Avoid vague CTAs like "Explore" or "Discover" unless they're leading to something specific.
- **Create Urgency:** People are more likely to act if they think they might miss out. Use time-limited offers, countdown timers, or exclusive deals to create a sense of urgency. "Only 5 left in stock" or "Sale ends at midnight" can push someone from just thinking about it to actually making a purchase.

2. Engage and Follow Up:

- **Stay in Touch:** Don't let the conversation end after someone's shown interest. Use email marketing, retargeting ads, or even personal follow-ups to keep the connection alive. A well-timed follow-up can be the difference between a lost lead and a loyal customer.
- **Reward Action:** Incentivize the next step with bonuses or discounts. For example, "Get 10% off your first purchase

when you sign up" not only encourages action but also builds your customer list for future marketing efforts.

Case Study: How Red Bull Keeps Everyone's Attention

Red Bull doesn't just sell energy drinks—they sell a lifestyle. From extreme sports sponsorships to the infamous "Stratos" jump from the edge of space, Red Bull creates spectacles that captivate global audiences. Their content isn't just about selling a product; it's about embodying the thrill-seeking, high-energy lifestyle their brand represents. This approach has made them a leader in both their industry and in content marketing.

Final Thoughts: Be Bold, Be Unforgettable

Attention isn't just about being seen—it's about making an impact that drives results. In a world where everyone is competing for the spotlight, you need to be the brand they can't ignore. Be bold, be memorable, and watch as that attention turns into profit.

Chapter 2:

Influence to Income: Turn Attention into Profit

Once you've successfully captured attention, the next crucial step is to convert that attention into income. Influence plays a pivotal role in this process. It's not just about being seen—it's about persuading your audience to take the next step and make a purchase. This chapter delves into how you can leverage your influence to transform attention into tangible profits.

The Psychology of Influence

Influence is deeply rooted in psychology. Understanding how people think and what motivates them to make decisions is key to turning interest into action. There are several psychological principles at play when it comes to influence:

1. **Reciprocity:** People are more likely to give when they have received something first. Offering value upfront—whether it's through free content, samples, or helpful advice—creates a sense of obligation that can lead to sales.
2. **Scarcity:** The less available something is, the more people want it. Limited-time offers, exclusive deals, or limited stock can create a sense of urgency that drives purchases.
3. **Social Proof:** People tend to follow the crowd. When potential customers see that others have purchased and are satisfied with your product, they're more likely to buy as well. Testimonials, reviews, and influencer endorsements are powerful tools for building social proof.

Key Techniques to Turn Influence into Income

1. Build Authority:

- **Be the Expert:** Position yourself as an authority in your niche. Create content that educates, informs, and adds value. When people view you as a trusted expert, they are more likely to purchase from you because they trust your recommendations.

2. Create a Sense of Urgency:

- **Act Now:** Encourage immediate action by using language and tactics that convey urgency. Phrases like "limited time only," "while supplies last," or "last chance" can motivate potential customers to buy now rather than later.

3. Use Clear Calls to Action (CTAs):

- **Guide Your Audience:** Make it easy for your audience to take the next step by using clear and direct calls to action. Whether it's "Buy Now," "Sign Up Today," or "Claim Your Discount," your CTA should leave no doubt about what the customer should do next.

4. Leverage Testimonials and Reviews:

- **Show Proof:** Highlight customer testimonials, case studies, and reviews prominently in your marketing materials. This social proof reassures potential buyers that they're making the right choice by purchasing your product or service.

Monetizing Your Influence

Turning influence into income isn't just about making a quick sale—it's about creating a sustainable revenue stream. Here's how to build long-term profitability through influence:

1. **Develop Multiple Income Streams:**
   - **Diversify:** Don't rely on just one product or service. Offer a range of options, from premium products to low-cost items, so you can appeal to different segments of your audience. Additionally, consider passive income streams such as affiliate marketing, online courses, or digital downloads.

2. **Upsell and Cross-Sell:**
   - **Increase Order Value:** Encourage customers to purchase additional items or upgrade their purchase. For example, if someone is buying a camera, suggest a lens or a carrying case as add-ons.

3. **Build a Loyal Customer Base:**
   - **Retain and Repeat:** Focus on customer retention by offering loyalty programs, regular discounts, and exclusive deals to repeat customers. A loyal customer base not only provides a steady income but also acts as a powerful advocate for your brand.

Case Study: The Rise of Kylie Jenner's Influence Empire

Kylie Jenner leveraged her massive social media following to launch Kylie Cosmetics, a billion-dollar beauty empire. By using her influence to promote her products directly to her millions of followers, she turned attention into significant profit. Her use of limited-edition product drops, influencer collaborations, and direct social media marketing are prime examples of how to convert influence into income effectively.

Final Thoughts: Influence Is Power

Influence, when harnessed correctly, can be one of the most powerful tools in your sales arsenal. By understanding the psychology behind influence and applying the right techniques, you can turn the attention you've captured into sustained, profitable growth. Remember, influence isn't just about making sales—it's about building trust, authority, and a loyal customer base that will continue to support your business in the long term

Chapter 3:
The Power of First Impressions

In sales, first impressions are everything. The moment you meet a prospect or client, they begin forming opinions about you and your brand. These initial judgments can significantly influence the outcome of your sales efforts, making it crucial to master the art of making a strong, positive first impression.

Why First Impressions Matter

First impressions are formed quickly, often within the first few seconds of an interaction. These impressions are based on a combination of factors, including appearance, body language, tone of voice, and communication skills. A positive first impression can set the tone for a successful relationship, while a negative one can be difficult to overcome, no matter how good your product or service may be.

Key Elements of a Strong First Impression

1. **Appearance and Presentation:**

- **Dress for Success:** Your appearance plays a significant role in how others perceive you. Dressing appropriately for the occasion shows that you respect the client and take the meeting seriously. Ensure that your clothing is clean, well-fitted, and aligned with the industry standards.
- **Personal Grooming:** Attention to personal grooming—such as neat hair, clean nails, and a fresh, professional look—further reinforces a positive image. It shows that you care about the details, which can translate into how you handle business.

2. **Body Language and Non-Verbal Cues:**
   - **Confident Posture:** Your posture can communicate confidence and competence. Stand or sit up straight, avoid slouching, and make sure your body language is open and approachable. Crossing your arms or looking down can signal disinterest or defensiveness.
   - **Eye Contact and Smile:** Maintaining good eye contact shows that you are engaged and trustworthy. A genuine smile can create a warm, welcoming atmosphere and make the other person feel at ease. These non-verbal cues are crucial in establishing a connection early on.

3. **Communication Skills:**
   - **Clear and Concise Language:** How you communicate is just as important as what you communicate. Speak clearly, avoid jargon that might confuse the client, and make sure your message is easy to understand. Clarity in communication builds trust and ensures that your message is received as intended.
   - **Active Listening:** First impressions aren't just about talking—they're also about listening. Show that you value the other person's input by actively listening to what they have to say. Nod, take notes if appropriate, and respond thoughtfully to their comments.

4. **Punctuality and Preparedness:**
   - **Be On Time:** Punctuality is a key factor in making a good first impression. Arriving late can give the impression that you're disorganized or don't value the other person's time. Aim to arrive a few minutes early to demonstrate reliability and respect.
   - **Come Prepared:** Being well-prepared for the meeting shows that you are serious and professional. Know the key points you want to discuss, have any necessary materials ready,

and be familiar with the client's background. Preparation demonstrates that you're invested in the interaction.

Real-World Example: The Impact of a First Impression

Imagine meeting a potential client for the first time. You arrive on time, dressed appropriately, and greet them with a warm smile and a firm handshake. Throughout the meeting, you maintain good eye contact, listen actively, and communicate your points clearly and confidently. By the end of the meeting, the client feels respected, understood, and positive about working with you—largely due to the strong first impression you've made.

Final Thoughts: Making First Impressions Count

First impressions are powerful and lasting. In sales, they can set the stage for a successful relationship or create obstacles that are difficult to overcome. By focusing on your appearance, body language, communication skills, and punctuality, you can ensure that your first impressions consistently leave a positive impact. Remember, you never get a second chance to make a first impression, so make it count every time.

Chapter 4:

Sell the Story, Not the Product

In the crowded marketplace, products and services are often similar in function and price. What sets them apart is the story behind them. This chapter explores how storytelling can transform the way you sell, making your products not just items for purchase but experiences and narratives that resonate deeply with customers.

The Power of Storytelling

Humans are wired to connect with stories. Stories evoke emotions, create connections, and make information more memorable. When you sell through storytelling, you're not just offering a product—you're offering a piece of your brand's narrative that customers can relate to, identify with, and share.

Crafting a Compelling Brand Story

1. **Identify Your Core Message:**

- **What's Your Purpose?:** Every story starts with a central message. For your brand, this might be your mission, the problem you solve, or the values you stand for. This message should be clear and resonate with your target audience.
- **The "Why":** Explain why your brand exists beyond making a profit. Simon Sinek's famous concept, "Start with Why," emphasizes that people don't buy what you do; they buy why you do it. Your "why" should be the cornerstone of your story.

2. **Highlight the Journey:**
   - **Overcoming Obstacles:** Share the challenges your brand has faced and how you overcame them. This not only humanizes your brand but also adds authenticity to your story. Customers appreciate knowing that behind the polished product is a journey of growth, struggle, and perseverance.
   - **The Evolution of Your Product:** Discuss how your product or service has evolved over time to meet customer needs better. This shows that you listen to your customers and are committed to continuous improvement.

3. **Use Relatable Characters:**
   - **Who's in Your Story?:** Every story needs characters, and in brand storytelling, these are often your customers, employees, or even yourself as the founder. Highlight how your product has made a difference in the lives of real people.
   - **Customer Testimonials:** Incorporate customer testimonials and case studies as part of your narrative. When potential customers see how others have benefited from your product, they can more easily envision themselves having a similar experience.

Using Storytelling to Drive Sales

Storytelling doesn't just make your brand memorable—it also drives sales by creating an emotional connection that encourages customers to take action.

1. **Align the Story with Your Audience's Values:**
   - **Know Your Audience:** Tailor your brand story to resonate with the specific values, beliefs, and needs of your target audience. When your story aligns with what matters to them,

they are more likely to feel a connection and choose your product over others.

2. **Call to Action with a Story:**
   - **Story-Based CTAs:** Instead of using generic calls to action, craft CTAs that are tied to your brand's story. For example, "Join us on our journey to make the world more sustainable—get your eco-friendly product today!" This approach ties the purchase directly to the narrative.

3. **Visual Storytelling:**
   - **Use Visuals:** In the digital age, visuals are a crucial part of storytelling. Use videos, infographics, and photos to tell your story in a way that's easy to digest and shareable. A well-produced video that tells your brand's story can be a powerful tool for attracting and converting customers.

Case Study: Nike's "Just Do It" Campaign

Nike's "Just Do It" campaign is a classic example of powerful storytelling. The campaign wasn't just about selling shoes—it was about inspiring people to push their limits and achieve greatness. The message resonated deeply with Nike's audience, making it one of the most successful marketing campaigns of all time. By aligning its brand story with the values of its customers, Nike didn't just sell shoes—they sold a lifestyle.

Final Thoughts: Stories Sell, Products Don't

In today's market, selling the product alone isn't enough. Customers want to connect with the brands they buy from, and storytelling is the bridge that creates that connection. By crafting a compelling narrative around your brand and products, you can transform the way you sell and build a loyal customer base that resonates with your story.

Chapter 5:
Build Trust, Build Loyalty, Generate Sales

Trust is the cornerstone of any successful business relationship. Without trust, no amount of marketing or sales tactics will yield long-term results. This chapter dives into the importance of building trust with your customers, how it translates to loyalty, and ultimately, how it drives sales.

Why Trust Matters

In an age where consumers are bombarded with options, trust is what sets your brand apart. Trust is built over time through consistent, reliable actions and communications. When customers trust your brand, they are more likely to be loyal, make repeat purchases, and recommend your products or services to others. This trust translates directly into sales and long-term business success.

Key Strategies to Build Trust

1. **Transparency and Honesty:**
   - **Open Communication:** Be upfront about your products, services, and policies. If there are limitations, don't hide them. Transparency builds credibility. For example, if you run an e-commerce business, clearly outline shipping times, costs, and return policies.
   - **Admit Mistakes:** If something goes wrong, acknowledge it quickly and take steps to rectify the situation. Customers appreciate honesty and will often forgive mistakes if they see that the company is committed to making things right.

2. **Consistency:**
   - **Deliver on Promises:** Ensure that your product or service consistently meets or exceeds customer expectations. Whether it's product quality, customer service, or delivery times, consistency builds reliability and trust.
   - **Brand Voice and Messaging:** Maintain a consistent brand voice and messaging across all channels, from social media to email marketing. Consistency in how you communicate with customers reinforces trust.

3. **Customer Engagement:**
   - **Listen and Respond:** Actively listen to customer feedback and engage with them across various platforms. Responding to comments, reviews, and messages shows that you value their input and are committed to their satisfaction.
   - **Personalization:** Tailor your interactions and offerings to individual customer preferences. Personalized experiences make customers feel valued and understood, further deepening their trust in your brand.

Turning Trust into Loyalty

Once trust is established, the next step is fostering customer loyalty. Loyal customers are not only more likely to make repeat purchases, but they are also more likely to become brand advocates, spreading positive word of mouth and bringing in new customers.

1. Loyalty Programs:

- **Rewards for Loyalty:** Implement a loyalty program that rewards repeat customers with discounts, exclusive offers, or points that can be redeemed for future purchases. This encourages continued patronage and strengthens the customer-brand relationship.

2. Exclusive Offers:

- **VIP Treatment:** Offer special deals or early access to new products for your most loyal customers. This makes them feel appreciated and valued, further reinforcing their loyalty.

3. Customer Appreciation:

- **Express Gratitude:** Show appreciation for your customers through thank-you notes, special gifts, or recognition in your communications. Simple gestures can go a long way in building a loyal customer base.

Case Study: How Amazon Builds Trust and Loyalty

Amazon is a prime example of a company that has built immense trust and loyalty among its customers. Through consistent delivery of products, transparent pricing, and a customer-centric approach, Amazon has earned the loyalty of millions. Their Prime membership program, which offers benefits like free shipping, exclusive deals, and access to entertainment, has further cemented customer loyalty by offering ongoing value.

Final Thoughts: Trust is the Foundation of Sales

Trust is not just a nice-to-have; it's a fundamental aspect of building a successful, sustainable business. By focusing on transparency, consistency, and customer engagement, you can build trust with your customers, foster loyalty, and ultimately drive sales. Remember, a loyal customer base is one of the most valuable assets any business can have.

Chapter 6:

Create Urgency: Make Them Buy Now

Creating a sense of urgency is one of the most effective sales strategies to encourage immediate action. When customers believe that an opportunity is fleeting, they're more likely to make a purchase decision quickly to avoid missing out. This chapter explores how to harness the power of urgency to drive sales.

Why Urgency Works

Urgency taps into the fear of missing out (FOMO). It creates a psychological trigger that compels people to act before it's too late. By limiting time or availability, you can motivate customers to prioritize purchasing your product or service over others.

Strategies to Create Urgency

1. **Time-Limited Offers:**

- **Flash Sales:** Offer discounts or special deals for a limited time, such as 24-hour flash sales. The short timeframe pushes customers to act quickly rather than waiting and potentially missing out.
- **Countdown Timers:** Use countdown timers on your website or in your emails to visually show how much time is left for a particular offer. This visual cue can significantly increase the sense of urgency.

2. **Scarcity Tactics:**
   - **Limited Stock:** Highlight the limited availability of a product. Phrases like "Only 3 left in stock" or "Limited edition" can prompt customers to buy now rather than risk the item being sold out.
   - **Exclusive Access:** Offer early access or exclusive deals to a select group of customers, such as VIPs or loyalty program members. This creates a sense of exclusivity and urgency to be part of the "in" crowd.

3. **Seasonal and Event-Based Urgency:**
   - **Holiday Sales:** Tie promotions to holidays or special events, such as Black Friday, Cyber Monday, or end-of-season sales. These events naturally create urgency as customers expect deals to be available for a limited time.
   - **Limited-Time Bundles:** Create product bundles that are only available for a short period. For example, a "Summer Essentials Kit" available only during the summer months can drive purchases from customers who want to take advantage of the seasonal offering.

4. **Incentives for Immediate Action:**
   - **Bonus Gifts:** Offer a free gift or bonus for customers who purchase within a certain timeframe. For example, "Buy in the next 2 hours and receive a free accessory!" This adds extra value and urgency to the purchase decision.
   - **Discount Expiration:** Offer a discount that expires soon, such as "Get 20% off today only." This encourages customers to take advantage of the deal immediately rather than postponing their purchase.

Avoiding Overuse of Urgency

While urgency is a powerful tool, overusing it can lead to customer fatigue and reduce its effectiveness. If customers feel that every offer is urgent, they may start to ignore them or become skeptical of the scarcity claims.

1. **Be Authentic:**
   - **Honesty Matters:** Ensure that your urgency tactics are genuine. Don't create false scarcity or use countdown timers that reset after the time expires. Customers can sense inauthenticity, which can damage trust in your brand.
   - **Balance Your Tactics:** Use urgency sparingly and strategically. Reserve it for special promotions or product launches to keep it effective and credible.

Case Study: How Amazon Leverages Urgency

Amazon is a master of creating urgency through its "Lightning Deals" and limited-time offers. These deals are prominently displayed with countdown timers, showing customers how much time they have left to snag a bargain. This approach effectively drives sales by making customers feel that they need to act quickly to secure the best price.

Final Thoughts: Urgency Drives Action

Urgency is a powerful motivator that can significantly boost sales when used correctly. By creating a sense of scarcity or time pressure, you can encourage customers to act quickly and make a purchase. However, it's important to use urgency authentically and strategically to maintain trust and credibility with your customers. When done right, urgency not only drives immediate sales but also enhances the overall customer experience by adding excitement and value.

Chapter 7:

Turn On Customer 'Oh No No' into 'Oh Yes Yes'

Objections are a natural part of the sales process, but they don't have to be roadblocks. This chapter focuses on how to effectively handle and overcome customer objections, turning potential "no's" into enthusiastic "yes's."

Understanding the Root of Objections

Objections usually stem from one of three concerns: price, value, or trust. By understanding the root cause of an objection, you can tailor your response to address the specific concern and alleviate the customer's hesitation.

Key Strategies to Overcome Objections

1. **Listen and Empathize:**

- **Hear Them Out:** Before jumping to a solution, take the time to listen to the customer's concerns. Show empathy by acknowledging their feelings and validating their perspective. This builds rapport and makes the customer feel heard.
- **Ask Questions:** Clarify the objection by asking open-ended questions. For example, "Can you tell me more about what's holding you back?" This allows you to get to the heart of the issue and address it effectively.

2. **Reframe the Objection:**

- **Shift the Perspective:** Turn the objection into a reason to buy. For instance, if a customer objects to the price, highlight the long-term value and potential cost savings of your product. Reframing helps the customer see the bigger picture and the benefits they might have overlooked.

3. **Provide Social Proof:**

   - **Show Success Stories:** Use testimonials, case studies, and reviews to demonstrate how other customers with similar objections found success with your product. Seeing how others overcame the same concerns can be a powerful motivator.
   - **Share Data and Facts:** If the objection is about performance or results, back up your claims with data and statistics. Hard evidence can help overcome skepticism and build trust.

4. **Offer a Risk-Free Trial:**

   - **Lower the Risk:** If a customer is hesitant, offer a risk-free trial, money-back guarantee, or demo. This reduces the perceived risk and gives the customer the confidence to move forward with the purchase.
   - **Highlight Satisfaction Guarantees:** Emphasize your commitment to customer satisfaction by offering guarantees or easy returns. This can alleviate concerns and make the decision to buy easier.

Turning Objections into Sales Opportunities

Objections aren't the end of the conversation—they're opportunities to learn more about your customer's needs and to demonstrate the value of your product. By approaching objections with confidence and empathy, you can turn potential barriers into stepping stones toward closing the sale.

Case Study: How Zappos Overcame the Objection of Buying Shoes Online

When Zappos first started, many customers were hesitant to buy shoes online because they couldn't try them on first. Zappos addressed this objection by offering free shipping and free returns, allowing customers to try on shoes at home with no risk. This approach not only overcame the objection but also built a reputation for excellent customer service, contributing to Zappos' success as a leading online retailer.

Final Thoughts: Objections as Opportunities

Handling objections effectively is a key skill in sales. Rather than seeing objections as obstacles, view them as opportunities to engage with your customer, provide additional value, and demonstrate the benefits of your product. With the right approach, you can turn every "no" into a "yes" and build stronger, more trusting customer relationships in the process.

Chapter 8:

Sell the Experience, Close the Deal: Master Emotional Selling

In today's competitive market, selling a product based solely on its features and benefits isn't enough. Customers are driven by emotions, and the experiences you create around your product can be the key to closing the deal. This chapter delves into the art of emotional selling and how to create memorable experiences that resonate with customers and lead to sales.

The Power of Emotional Selling

Emotions drive decisions. Whether it's the excitement of getting a great deal, the joy of owning something exclusive, or the relief of solving a problem, emotions play a crucial role in the buying process. By tapping into these emotions, you can create a deeper connection with your customers and motivate them to take action.

Strategies for Selling the Experience

1. **Understand the Customer's Emotional Triggers:**

- **Identify Pain Points:** Before you can sell the solution, you need to understand the customer's problem. What are their pain points? What frustrations are they trying to overcome? By identifying these emotional triggers, you can tailor your messaging to address their specific needs.
- **Highlight Aspirations:** What does the customer aspire to achieve? Whether it's personal success, a better lifestyle, or peace of mind, aligning your product with these aspirations can create a powerful emotional connection.

2. **Create a Memorable Buying Experience:**
   - **Engage the Senses:** A memorable buying experience engages the senses. Whether it's through a visually appealing website, a luxurious in-store environment, or the tactile experience of your product, engaging the senses can evoke emotions that enhance the overall experience.
   - **Personalize the Interaction:** Personalization goes a long way in creating a positive emotional experience. Address customers by name, tailor recommendations to their preferences, and make them feel valued. Personalized experiences make customers feel special and increase their emotional attachment to your brand.

3. **Use Storytelling to Evoke Emotions:**
   - **Craft a Narrative:** Stories are powerful tools for evoking emotions. Share stories that highlight how your product has improved the lives of others, solved problems, or made a difference. A well-crafted narrative can make customers see themselves in the story and feel the emotions associated with it.
   - **Showcase Real-Life Examples:** Use testimonials, case studies, or user-generated content to showcase real-life examples of how your product has positively impacted others. Seeing real people benefit from your product can create a sense of trust and inspire similar emotions in potential customers.

4. **Build Anticipation and Excitement:**
   - **Pre-Launch Buzz:** If you're launching a new product, build anticipation by teasing its features, benefits, and launch date. Creating a sense of excitement and urgency can lead to eager customers who are emotionally invested in being among the first to own your product.

- **Limited Editions and Exclusivity:** Offering limited editions or exclusive deals can create a sense of urgency and excitement. Customers who feel they are part of something special are more likely to make an emotional purchase.

Turning Emotional Selling into Sales

Once you've tapped into the customer's emotions, the next step is to guide them towards making a purchase. Here's how to do it effectively:

1. **Align Emotions with Action:**

- **Call to Action with Emotion:** Your call to action (CTA) should align with the emotions you've evoked. For example, if your product offers peace of mind, your CTA could be "Experience peace of mind today—buy now!" Aligning the CTA with the emotional benefits reinforces the decision to purchase.

2. **Overcome Objections with Empathy:**

- **Address Concerns:** If a customer hesitates, address their concerns with empathy. For instance, if they're worried about the cost, emphasize the long-term emotional benefits of the purchase, such as the joy or security it will bring. Empathy helps build trust and makes customers feel understood.

3. **Follow Up with a Positive Experience:**

- **After-Sales Support:** The emotional experience doesn't end with the sale. Ensure that your after-sales support continues to evoke positive emotions, whether through follow-up emails, customer service, or loyalty programs. A positive post-purchase experience can lead to repeat business and referrals.

Case Study: How Disney Sells the Magic

Disney is a master of emotional selling. From the moment you enter a Disney park, you're immersed in a magical experience that taps into emotions of wonder, joy, and nostalgia. Disney doesn't just sell tickets to a theme park—they sell the promise of creating lifelong memories. By focusing on the emotional experience, Disney has built a brand that customers are willing to pay a premium for, time and time again.

Final Thoughts: Emotions Close Deals

In the world of sales, emotions are powerful motivators. By understanding your customers' emotional triggers and creating experiences that resonate with those emotions, you can build stronger connections, close more deals, and foster long-term loyalty. Remember, it's not just about what you're selling—it's about how you make your customers feel.

Chapter 9:

Loyalty Goldmine: Keep Them Coming Back

Customer loyalty is the holy grail of business success. Loyal customers not only bring in repeat business, but they also become advocates for your brand, driving referrals and enhancing your reputation. This chapter focuses on strategies to build and maintain customer loyalty, turning one-time buyers into lifelong fans.

Why Loyalty Matters

Loyal customers are more profitable than new customers. They're easier to sell to, less sensitive to price changes, and more likely to recommend your products or services to others. Building loyalty isn't just about providing a good product—it's about creating a relationship that customers value and want to maintain.

Key Strategies to Build Customer Loyalty

1. Deliver Exceptional Customer Service:

- **Go Above and Beyond:** Exceptional customer service is the cornerstone of customer loyalty. Ensure that every interaction with your customers is positive, whether it's answering questions, resolving issues, or providing support. Going the extra mile can turn a satisfied customer into a loyal one.
- **Be Responsive:** Quick and effective responses to customer inquiries and concerns demonstrate that you value their time and business. Whether through phone, email, or social media, ensure that your customer service is accessible and responsive.

2. **Create a Loyalty Program:**
   - **Reward Loyalty:** Implement a loyalty program that rewards customers for repeat purchases. This could be in the form of points, discounts, or exclusive offers. A well-designed loyalty program not only incentivizes repeat business but also makes customers feel valued.
   - **Tiered Rewards:** Consider offering tiered rewards that increase in value the more a customer spends. This encourages customers to spend more to unlock higher-level rewards, deepening their loyalty to your brand.

3. **Personalize the Experience:**
   - **Know Your Customers:** Use data to understand your customers' preferences, behaviors, and needs. Personalize your communications, offers, and recommendations to make each customer feel like they're receiving special treatment.
   - **Tailored Offers:** Send personalized offers or discounts based on past purchases or browsing behavior. For example, if a customer frequently buys a particular type of product, offer them a discount on a related item. Personalization fosters a sense of connection and loyalty.

4. **Engage and Build a Community:**
   - **Foster Connections:** Create a community around your brand where customers can connect with each other and share their experiences. This could be through social media groups, online forums, or in-person events. A strong community fosters a sense of belonging and loyalty.
   - **User-Generated Content:** Encourage customers to share their experiences with your product through photos, videos, or reviews. Featuring this content on your platforms not only engages your customers but also shows that you value their input.

5. **Show Appreciation:**
   - **Thank Your Customers:** Regularly express your appreciation for your customers. This could be through thank-you notes, surprise gifts, or exclusive access to new products or events. A little appreciation goes a long way in making customers feel valued and loyal.
   - **Celebrate Milestones:** Recognize and celebrate customer milestones, such as anniversaries of their first purchase or reaching a certain spending threshold. Personalized recognition reinforces the customer's connection to your brand.

Turning Loyalty into Advocacy

Loyal customers don't just buy from you—they advocate for you. Turning loyalty into advocacy involves encouraging satisfied customers to spread the word about your brand, whether through referrals, reviews, or social media.

1. **Referral Programs:**
   - **Reward Referrals:** Implement a referral program that rewards customers for bringing in new business. Offer discounts, freebies, or loyalty points to customers who refer friends and family. This not only encourages loyalty but also helps you acquire new customers at a lower cost.
   - **Make It Easy:** Ensure that your referral process is simple and easy to share. Provide customers with referral links, codes, or social media share buttons to make it effortless for them to recommend your brand.

2. **Encourage Reviews and Testimonials:**
   - **Ask for Feedback:** Regularly ask satisfied customers to leave reviews or provide testimonials. Positive reviews not

only enhance your credibility but also serve as powerful social proof for potential customers.
- **Feature Advocates:** Showcase your most loyal customers and their stories on your website, social media, or marketing materials. Featuring your advocates not only rewards them but also inspires others to become advocates themselves.

Case Study: Starbucks' Loyalty Program Success

Starbucks has built one of the most successful loyalty programs in the retail industry. The Starbucks Rewards program offers customers points for every purchase, which can be redeemed for free drinks, food, and exclusive offers. The program also includes tiered rewards, personalized offers, and early access to new products. By focusing on customer loyalty, Starbucks has not only increased repeat business but also fostered a community of brand advocates who promote the brand through word-of-mouth and social media.

Final Thoughts: Loyalty is a Goldmine

Customer loyalty is one of the most valuable assets a business can have. By delivering exceptional service, personalizing the customer experience, and showing appreciation, you can build a loyal customer base that not only keeps coming back but also becomes a powerful advocate for your brand. Remember, loyalty isn't just about repeat business—it's about creating lasting relationships that drive growth and long-term success.

Chapter 10:

Upsell Like a Boss: Boost Sales

Upselling is a powerful technique that can significantly increase the average order value and boost your overall sales. When done correctly, it not only benefits your business but also enhances the customer's experience by offering them additional value. This chapter explores strategies for mastering the art of upselling without coming across as pushy or overbearing.

Understanding Upselling

Upselling involves encouraging customers to purchase a more expensive item, an add-on, or an upgrade. The key to successful upselling is to focus on providing additional value to the customer rather than just pushing for a higher sale. When customers feel that the upsell enhances their experience or better meets their needs, they are more likely to accept it.

Strategies for Effective Upselling

1. **Know Your Products Inside and Out:**

- **Product Knowledge is Power:** To upsell effectively, you need to have a deep understanding of your products and how they complement each other. This allows you to make personalized recommendations that genuinely add value to the customer's purchase.
- **Match the Upsell to the Customer's Needs:** Tailor your upsell offers based on the customer's specific needs and preferences. For example, if a customer is buying a laptop, suggest an extended warranty or a higher-performance model that better suits their usage.

2. **Timing is Everything:**
   - **Strategic Timing:** Offer the upsell at a moment when the customer is already inclined to buy, such as during the checkout process. This is when they are most committed and open to suggestions that enhance their purchase.
   - **Avoid Overwhelming the Customer:** Don't bombard the customer with too many upsell options at once. Focus on a few key upsells that align with their initial purchase and add clear value.

3. **Use Bundling and Packaging:**
   - **Create Value Bundles:** Bundle complementary products together at a slightly discounted rate compared to buying each item separately. For example, offering a camera with a lens, memory card, and carrying case as a bundle can be more appealing than selling each item individually.
   - **Tiered Packages:** Offer tiered versions of your product or service (e.g., basic, premium, deluxe) that gradually increase in value and price. This gives customers the flexibility to choose the option that best meets their needs while encouraging them to consider higher-priced tiers.

4. **Leverage Data and Personalization:**
   - **Personalized Recommendations:** Use customer data and purchase history to make personalized upsell recommendations. For example, if a customer frequently buys skincare products, suggest a premium version or an add-on like a serum or face mask that complements their routine.
   - **Dynamic Upselling:** Implement dynamic upselling techniques on your e-commerce site by displaying related products or "frequently bought together" items on product pages and during checkout.

Overcoming Resistance to Upselling

Customers may sometimes resist upselling attempts, especially if they perceive it as pushy or unnecessary. Here's how to overcome this resistance:

1. **Focus on Benefits, Not Features:**
   - **Highlight the Value:** Instead of simply listing the features of the upsell, focus on how it benefits the customer. Explain how the upgrade or additional product will enhance their experience or solve a specific problem.
   - **Customer-Centric Approach:** Frame the upsell as a way to improve the customer's satisfaction and ensure they're getting the most out of their purchase.

2. **Offer a Risk-Free Trial:**
   - **Try Before You Buy:** If possible, offer a risk-free trial or a satisfaction guarantee on the upsell. This reduces the customer's perceived risk and makes them more likely to accept the offer.
   - **Money-Back Guarantee:** Offering a money-back guarantee on upsells can reassure customers that they're making a risk-free decision, which can increase acceptance rates.

Case Study: Amazon's Upselling and Cross-Selling Mastery

Amazon is renowned for its upselling and cross-selling strategies. From the "Customers who bought this item also bought" recommendations to the "Frequently bought together" bundles, Amazon seamlessly integrates upselling into the shopping experience. These techniques have not only boosted Amazon's average order value but also enhanced the customer experience by providing relevant and valuable suggestions.

Final Thoughts: Upselling for Success

Upselling, when done right, is a win-win for both the business and the customer. It boosts your sales and profitability while enhancing the customer's experience by offering them greater value. The key is to be customer-centric, timing your offers appropriately, and focusing on the benefits that the upsell provides. With the right approach, upselling can become a natural and effective part of your sales strategy.

Chapter 11:

Networking: The Hidden Key to Sales Success

In the world of sales, who you know can be just as important as what you know. Networking is an invaluable tool that can open doors to new opportunities, partnerships, and customers. This chapter explores the importance of networking in sales and provides strategies to build and leverage a powerful network that drives business success.

The Power of Networking

Networking is more than just exchanging business cards at events—it's about building genuine relationships that can lead to long-term business success. A strong network provides you with access to valuable resources, insights, and referrals that can significantly boost your sales efforts.

Strategies to Build a Strong Network

1. **Be Authentic:**

- **Build Genuine Relationships:** Networking is not about making superficial connections; it's about building meaningful, long-term relationships. Approach networking with the mindset of helping others and adding value, rather than just seeking what you can gain.
- **Show Interest:** Take the time to learn about the people you meet. Ask questions, listen actively, and show genuine interest in their work and challenges. This builds trust and lays the foundation for a strong, reciprocal relationship.

2. **Leverage Online Platforms:**
   - **Utilize LinkedIn:** LinkedIn is a powerful tool for networking with professionals in your industry. Join relevant groups, participate in discussions, and connect with influencers and potential partners. Regularly share valuable content to establish yourself as a thought leader in your field.
   - **Engage on Social Media:** Engage with your network on platforms like Twitter, Instagram, or industry-specific forums. Share insights, comment on posts, and contribute to conversations to stay top of mind with your connections.

3. **Attend Industry Events:**
   - **Join Conferences and Trade Shows:** Attending industry events, conferences, and trade shows is an excellent way to meet new contacts and strengthen existing relationships. Be prepared with your elevator pitch and business cards, and focus on making quality connections rather than collecting as many cards as possible.
   - **Host or Participate in Workshops:** Hosting or participating in workshops or panels can position you as an expert in your field. It also provides an opportunity to network with other speakers, organizers, and attendees who are interested in your area of expertise.

4. **Follow Up Consistently:**
   - **Stay in Touch:** The key to effective networking is consistent follow-up. After meeting someone new, send a personalized message to express your interest in staying connected. Regularly check in with your network, whether it's through a quick email, a LinkedIn message, or a coffee catch-up.
   - **Offer Value:** Keep your network engaged by offering value, such as sharing relevant articles, providing introductions, or

offering your expertise. This shows that you're invested in the relationship and not just seeking something for yourself.

Leveraging Your Network for Sales Success

1. **Ask for Referrals:**

- **Leverage Connections:** Don't be afraid to ask your network for referrals. If you've built strong relationships, people will be more than willing to introduce you to potential clients or partners who could benefit from your product or service.

Referral Programs: Consider implementing a formal referral program that incentivizes your network to refer new business to you. This could include offering discounts, bonuses, or other rewards for successful referrals.

2. **Collaborate and Partner:**

- **Strategic Partnerships:** Look for opportunities to collaborate with others in your network. This could involve co-hosting events, creating joint marketing campaigns, or bundling complementary products or services. Partnerships can help you reach a broader audience and drive more sales.
- **Cross-Promotions:** Collaborate with non-competing businesses in your network to cross-promote each other's products or services. For example, if you sell fitness equipment, partner with a nutritionist or a fitness trainer to offer a bundled package.

3. **Seek Mentorship and Guidance:**

- **Learn from Others:** Networking isn't just about selling—it's also about learning. Seek out mentors and advisors within your network who can provide guidance, share their experiences, and help you navigate challenges in your sales journey.

- **Give Back:** As you progress in your career, look for opportunities to mentor others within your network. Helping others succeed not only strengthens your relationships but also enhances your reputation as a leader and expert in your field.

Case Study: How Networking Fueled the Success of Salesforce

Salesforce, a global leader in customer relationship management (CRM) software, leveraged networking to fuel its rapid growth. Marc Benioff, the founder of Salesforce, actively built relationships with industry leaders, investors, and potential customers through strategic networking. By aligning himself with influential figures and gaining their support, Benioff was able to propel Salesforce to become a dominant force in the CRM industry.

Final Thoughts: Networking is Your Secret Weapon

In the competitive world of sales, networking is your secret weapon. By building and nurturing a strong network, you gain access to valuable opportunities, insights, and resources that can accelerate your success. Remember, networking is not just about what you can get—it's about building mutually beneficial relationships that stand the test of time.

Chapter 12:

Close with Confidence: Seal the Deal

Closing a sale is often the most challenging part of the sales process, but it's also the most crucial. The ability to close with confidence separates successful salespeople from the rest. This chapter focuses on the techniques and mindset needed to effectively close deals and turn prospects into customers.

The Mindset of a Successful Closer

Confidence is key when it comes to closing a sale. Customers can sense hesitation or uncertainty, and it can make them second-guess their decision. To close with confidence, you need to believe in your product, understand your customer's needs, and approach the close with the expectation of success.

Effective Closing Techniques

1. **The Assumptive Close:**

- **Act as if the Sale is Inevitable:** The assumptive close involves acting as though the customer has already decided to buy. This can be done by asking questions like, "When would you like delivery?" or "Shall we set up your account today?" This technique subtly nudges the customer towards finalizing the purchase.
- **Stay Positive:** Maintain a positive attitude and speak as if the sale is a foregone conclusion. This confidence can be contagious, helping to alleviate any last-minute doubts the customer may have.

2. **The Urgency Close:**

- **Create a Sense of Urgency:** The urgency close leverages the customer's fear of missing out (FOMO). Highlight time-sensitive offers, limited availability, or upcoming price

increases to encourage immediate action. For example, "This discount is only available until the end of the day—would you like to take advantage of it now?"
- **Be Genuine:** Ensure that the urgency you create is genuine. Customers can detect when urgency is fabricated, which can damage trust and jeopardize the sale.

3. **The Summary Close:**

- **Recap the Benefits:** The summary close involves summarizing the key benefits and features of your product or service before asking for the sale. This reinforces the value you've provided and reminds the customer why they were interested in the first place. For example, "Just to recap, with this software, you'll save 10 hours a week on administrative tasks and increase your team's productivity by 20%. Are you ready to move forward?"
- **Address Final Objections:** As you summarize, be prepared to address any last-minute objections. Offer reassurances or additional information to help the customer feel confident in their decision.

4. **The Direct Close:**

- **Ask for the Sale:** Sometimes, the most effective approach is simply to ask for the sale directly. This technique works well when the customer has shown strong interest and all objections have been addressed. For example, "Are you ready to place your order today?" or "Can we go ahead and finalize the paperwork?"
- **Stay Calm and Confident:** The direct close requires a calm and confident demeanor. If you hesitate or appear uncertain, the customer may pick up on it and hesitate as well.

Handling Last-Minute Objections

Even at the closing stage, customers may raise last-minute objections. Handling these objections effectively can mean the difference between closing the deal and losing it.

1. **Stay Composed:**

   - **Keep Your Cool:** If a customer raises an objection, stay composed and don't react defensively. A calm and professional response shows that you're confident in your product and willing to address any concerns.
   - **Listen Carefully:** Take the time to fully understand the objection before responding. This shows that you value the customer's concerns and are committed to finding a solution.

2. **Reiterate the Value:**

   - **Reinforce the Benefits:** When addressing an objection, reiterate the key benefits of your product or service. For example, if the customer is concerned about cost, emphasize the long-term savings or return on investment they can expect.
   - **Provide Social Proof:** Use testimonials or case studies to demonstrate how other customers with similar concerns found success with your product. Seeing others overcome the same objections can reassure the customer.

Case Study: How HubSpot Masters the Close

HubSpot, a leading provider of inbound marketing and sales software, is known for its ability to close deals effectively. HubSpot's sales team uses a combination of assumptive closes, urgency, and personalized follow-up to convert leads into customers. By focusing on the customer's needs and providing ongoing value, HubSpot has built a reputation for closing deals with confidence and integrity.

Final Thoughts: Confidence Closes Deals

Closing a sale requires confidence, skill, and the ability to address last-minute objections. By mastering a variety of closing techniques, staying composed, and reinforcing the value of your product, you can close deals with confidence and achieve consistent sales success. Remember, the close is not just the end of the sales process—it's the beginning of a successful customer relationship.

Chapter 13:

Emotional Intelligence in Sales: Connecting on a Deeper Level

Sales isn't just about products or prices; it's about people. The most successful sales professionals understand that emotions drive decisions. Emotional intelligence (EQ) is the key to connecting with customers, building trust, and ultimately closing more deals.

The Role of Emotional Intelligence

EQ is the ability to understand and manage your own emotions while also recognizing and influencing the emotions of others. In sales, this translates to reading the room, understanding the unspoken needs of your customers, and responding in ways that build rapport and trust.

Components of Emotional Intelligence in Sales

1. **Self-Awareness**

- **Recognize Your Emotions:** Before you can connect with others, you need to understand yourself. Recognize your emotional triggers and how they influence your behavior during sales interactions.
- **Stay Grounded:** Maintain composure, especially in high-pressure situations. Your calmness and confidence can put customers at ease, making them more open to your proposals.

2. **Empathy**

- **Understand the Customer's Perspective:** Empathy is about seeing the situation from the customer's point of view. This doesn't mean agreeing with everything they say, but it does

mean understanding their concerns and addressing them in a way that feels genuine.
- **Respond to Their Emotions:** If a customer is frustrated, acknowledge their feelings before diving into solutions. This can defuse tension and pave the way for a more productive conversation.

3. **Social Skills**
- **Build Relationships:** Sales is about building relationships, not just closing deals. Take the time to get to know your customers on a personal level. This not only makes them more likely to buy but also more likely to return.
- **Influence with Integrity:** Use your social skills to influence outcomes positively. Whether it's guiding a hesitant customer towards a purchase or negotiating terms, do so with integrity and a focus on long-term relationships.

Real-Life Example: How EQ Transformed a Sales Team at Zappos

At Zappos, customer service reps are trained extensively in emotional intelligence. This training allows them to connect deeply with customers, often going above and beyond to meet their needs. The result? Unmatched customer loyalty and word-of-mouth marketing that has helped Zappos grow exponentially.

Final Thoughts: Selling with Heart

In a world of data and automation, emotional intelligence is what makes the difference between a good salesperson and a great one. By connecting with customers on a deeper level, you not only close more deals but also build relationships that last. Selling with heart isn't just good ethics—it's good business.

Chapter 14:

Cash Control: Master Your Money and Grow Your Wealth

Effective cash management is the backbone of any successful business. Without proper cash control, even profitable businesses can struggle to survive. This chapter focuses on strategies to master your money, optimize cash flow, and ensure long-term financial stability and growth.

The Importance of Cash Flow Management

Cash flow is the lifeblood of your business. It represents the money that comes in and goes out of your business over a specific period. Positive cash flow allows you to meet your obligations, reinvest in your business, and build a financial cushion for future growth. Negative cash flow, on the other hand, can lead to financial difficulties, even if your business is profitable on paper.

Key Strategies for Effective Cash Control

1. **Monitor Cash Flow Regularly:**

- **Keep Track:** Regularly monitor your cash flow to ensure that your business has enough liquidity to meet its obligations. Use cash flow statements and forecasts to track your inflows and outflows, identify trends, and anticipate future cash needs.
- **Set Up Alerts:** Set up alerts in your accounting software to notify you of significant changes in cash flow, such as unexpected expenses or late payments. This allows you to take action quickly before issues escalate.

2. **Optimize Receivables and Payables:**
   - **Speed Up Receivables:** Encourage customers to pay on time by offering incentives for early payments, such as discounts. Consider implementing automated invoicing and payment reminders to reduce delays in receiving payments.
   - **Manage Payables Efficiently:** Negotiate favorable payment terms with suppliers, such as extended payment deadlines or discounts for early payment. This helps you maintain positive cash flow while managing your liabilities effectively.

3. **Maintain a Cash Reserve:**
   - **Build a Safety Net:** Set aside a portion of your profits as a cash reserve to cover unexpected expenses or slow periods. A healthy cash reserve provides peace of mind and ensures that your business can weather financial challenges.
   - **Plan for Seasonal Fluctuations:** If your business experiences seasonal fluctuations, plan your cash flow accordingly. Save during peak periods to cover expenses during slower months.

4. **Control Costs and Expenses:**
   - **Review Expenses Regularly:** Regularly review your business expenses to identify areas where you can cut costs without compromising quality. This could include renegotiating contracts, finding more cost-effective suppliers, or eliminating unnecessary expenses.
   - **Invest in Efficiency:** Consider investing in technology or processes that improve efficiency and reduce costs in the long run. For example, automating routine tasks can save time and money, allowing you to allocate resources more effectively.

Maximizing Cash Flow for Growth

Once you've established strong cash flow management practices, the next step is to use your positive cash flow to fuel business growth.

1. **Reinvest in Your Business:**

- **Fund Growth Initiatives:** Use your cash flow to fund growth initiatives, such as expanding your product line, increasing marketing efforts, or entering new markets. Reinvesting profits into your business helps you build momentum and achieve long-term success.
- **Upgrade Equipment and Technology:** Invest in new equipment, technology, or software that can enhance productivity and efficiency. This not only improves your operations but also positions your business for future growth.

2. **Expand Your Cash Flow Streams:**

- **Diversify Revenue Streams:** Explore opportunities to diversify your revenue streams, such as introducing new products or services, targeting different customer segments, or expanding into new geographic areas. Diversification reduces risk and increases your business's resilience.
- **Leverage Financing Options:** If you need additional capital to fund growth, consider financing options such as business loans, lines of credit, or investor funding. Ensure that any financing you secure aligns with your cash flow needs and repayment capacity.

Case Study: How Amazon Manages Cash Flow for Growth

Amazon is a prime example of a company that has mastered cash flow management to fuel rapid growth. By optimizing its supply chain, negotiating favorable payment terms with suppliers, and reinvesting profits into new ventures, Amazon has consistently maintained positive cash flow. This financial discipline has enabled Amazon to expand its operations, acquire new businesses, and become one of the most valuable companies in the world.

Final Thoughts: Master Your Cash, Master Your Future

Effective cash control is essential for the survival and growth of your business. By monitoring cash flow, optimizing receivables and payables, and maintaining a cash reserve, you can ensure financial stability and position your business for long-term success. Remember, cash is king, and mastering your money is the key to building a sustainable and prosperous future for your business.

Chapter 15:

Scaling Your Business: Grow Big, Scale Fast

Scaling a business is both an exciting and challenging endeavor. It's about expanding your operations, reaching more customers, and increasing revenue—all while maintaining the quality and efficiency that made your business successful in the first place. This chapter focuses on the strategies and considerations needed to scale your business effectively and sustainably.

The Fundamentals of Scaling

Scaling isn't just about growing; it's about growing efficiently. As you scale, you'll encounter new challenges, including managing increased demand, maintaining product quality, and ensuring that your business infrastructure can handle the expansion. To scale successfully, you need a solid foundation and a clear strategy.

Key Strategies for Scaling Your Business

1. **Standardize Processes:**

- **Streamline Operations:** Before scaling, ensure that your business processes are standardized and streamlined. This includes everything from production and inventory management to customer service and order fulfillment. Standardized processes allow you to scale more efficiently without sacrificing quality or consistency.
- **Document Procedures:** Create detailed documentation for all critical processes. This not only helps in training new employees as you scale but also ensures that your

operations remain consistent across different locations or teams.

2. **Invest in Technology:**
   - **Automate Where Possible:** Technology plays a crucial role in scaling. Invest in automation tools and software that can handle repetitive tasks, such as invoicing, inventory management, and customer relationship management (CRM). Automation reduces the risk of errors and frees up your team to focus on higher-value activities.
   - **Scalable Infrastructure:** Choose technology solutions that can scale with your business. For example, cloud-based software allows you to easily increase storage or processing power as your business grows without the need for significant upfront investment in hardware.

3. **Build a Strong Team:**
   - **Hire for Growth:** As you scale, you'll need to build a team that can support your expansion. Hire employees who are not only skilled but also adaptable and aligned with your company's culture and values. A strong team is essential for maintaining quality and driving growth.
   - **Delegate and Empower:** As your business grows, it's important to delegate responsibilities and empower your team to make decisions. Trusting your team and giving them the autonomy to solve problems allows you to focus on strategic growth initiatives.

4. **Expand Your Market Reach:**
   - **Target New Markets:** Consider expanding into new geographic regions, industries, or customer segments. Conduct market research to identify areas with high growth potential and tailor your marketing and sales strategies to meet the needs of these new markets.

- **Diversify Your Product Line:** Expanding your product or service offerings can help you reach a broader audience and increase revenue streams. Ensure that any new products or services align with your brand and meet customer needs.

5. **Secure Financing for Growth:**

- **Explore Funding Options:** Scaling often requires additional capital. Explore various funding options, such as bank loans, venture capital, or crowdfunding, to finance your growth. Choose a funding option that aligns with your business goals and cash flow needs.
- **Manage Cash Flow:** As you scale, it's essential to maintain strong cash flow management. Ensure that you have enough liquidity to cover increased expenses and invest in growth opportunities. Regularly review your financial statements and forecasts to stay on top of your cash flow.

Managing the Challenges of Scaling

Scaling a business comes with its own set of challenges, including maintaining quality, managing increased complexity, and ensuring that your infrastructure can handle the growth.

1. **Maintain Quality Control:**

- **Set Quality Standards:** As you scale, it's important to maintain the quality of your products or services. Establish clear quality control standards and regularly monitor performance to ensure that these standards are being met.
- **Customer Feedback:** Use customer feedback to identify areas for improvement and address any quality issues promptly. Satisfied customers are essential for sustaining growth and building a positive reputation.

2. **Manage Complexity:**
   - **Simplify Where Possible:** Scaling often leads to increased complexity, whether in operations, supply chain management, or customer service. Look for opportunities to simplify processes and reduce unnecessary complexity. This could involve streamlining your product line, reducing the number of suppliers, or implementing more efficient communication tools.
   - **Implement Effective Communication:** As your team grows, effective communication becomes even more critical. Implement communication tools and practices that keep everyone aligned and informed, regardless of location or department.

3. **Adapt to Change:**
   - **Be Agile:** The business environment is constantly changing, and your ability to adapt is key to successful scaling. Stay agile and be prepared to pivot your strategy in response to market trends, customer needs, or new opportunities.
   - **Continuous Improvement:** Foster a culture of continuous improvement within your organization. Encourage employees to identify areas for improvement and experiment with new ideas and processes. This mindset of constant evolution will help your business stay competitive as it scales.

Case Study: How Airbnb Scaled Globally

Airbnb is a prime example of a company that scaled rapidly while maintaining quality and customer satisfaction. By leveraging technology, building a strong community of hosts and guests, and expanding into new markets, Airbnb was able to grow from a small startup to a global hospitality giant. The company's focus on standardizing processes, automating operations, and adapting to changing market conditions has been key to its success.

Final Thoughts: Scaling for Success

Scaling your business is an exciting journey, but it requires careful planning, strong leadership, and a commitment to maintaining quality and efficiency. By standardizing processes, investing in technology, building a strong team, and managing the challenges of growth, you can scale your business successfully and achieve your long-term goals. Remember, scaling is not just about growing bigger—it's about growing smarter and more sustainably.

Chapter 16:

Nail the Close: Finish Strong and Seal the Deal

The closing stage is where all your hard work pays off. It's the moment of truth when the customer decides whether or not to make the purchase. This chapter focuses on strategies to finish strong and seal the deal, ensuring that your sales efforts result in a successful close.

The Importance of a Strong Finish

No matter how well you've managed the sales process up to this point, the close is where you either win or lose the sale. A strong finish requires confidence, skill, and the ability to read the customer's signals. By mastering the art of closing, you can increase your conversion rates and build lasting customer relationships.

Techniques to Nail the Close

1. **The Trial Close:**

- **Test the Waters:** The trial close involves asking questions that gauge the customer's readiness to buy, without directly asking for the sale. For example, "How do you feel about the proposal so far?" or "Does this solution meet your needs?" This helps you assess whether the customer is ready to move forward or if there are any remaining concerns to address.
- **Identify Objections Early:** The trial close allows you to identify any objections early, so you can address them before making the final ask. This increases the likelihood of a smooth close when the time comes.

2. **The Ben Franklin Close:**
   - **Pros and Cons:** Named after Benjamin Franklin, who famously used this method to make decisions, the Ben Franklin close involves listing the pros and cons of the purchase decision. Present the list to the customer, highlighting the overwhelming benefits and minimizing the drawbacks. This technique helps the customer see the value of the purchase more clearly and can push them towards a positive decision.
   - **Collaborative Approach:** Involve the customer in creating the list. This collaborative approach makes them feel more in control of the decision-making process and more comfortable with the final choice.

3. **The Sharp Angle Close:**
   - **Turn Objections into Closures:** The sharp angle close is used when a customer presents an objection that you can easily address. For example, if a customer says, "I like the product, but I need a discount," you can respond with, "If I can offer you a 10% discount, will you move forward with the purchase today?" This technique turns objections into opportunities to close the sale.
   - **Be Prepared:** To use this technique effectively, you need to be prepared with solutions to common objections, such as discounts, additional features, or flexible payment terms.

4. **The Question Close:**
   - **Guide the Customer to the Answer:** The question close involves asking a series of questions that guide the customer to realize that the purchase is the right decision. For example, "Do you feel this product will solve your problem?" or "Would you like to start enjoying these benefits today?" By leading the customer to answer

positively, you make it easier for them to say "yes" to the final purchase.
- **Avoid Pressuring:** This technique should be used carefully to avoid pressuring the customer. The goal is to guide them to their own conclusion, not to force a decision.

Reading the Customer's Signals

1. **Verbal Cues:**
- **Positive Language:** Listen for positive language that indicates the customer is ready to buy, such as "That sounds great," "I can see how this would work," or "What's the next step?" These cues suggest that the customer is leaning towards a decision and is open to closing the deal.
- **Questions About Logistics:** If the customer starts asking about logistics, such as delivery times, payment options, or installation details, it's a strong signal that they're ready to move forward.
2. **Non-Verbal Cues:**
- **Body Language:** Pay attention to the customer's body language. Leaning forward, nodding, or making eye contact are positive signs that they're engaged and interested in closing the deal.
- **Pause in Conversation:** If the customer pauses and appears to be in deep thought, they may be internally weighing the decision. This is a crucial moment to reinforce the benefits and gently prompt for the close.

Overcoming Last-Minute Objections

1. **Stay Composed:**
- **Keep Your Cool:** If a customer raises an objection, stay composed and don't react defensively. A calm and professional response shows that you're confident in your product and willing to address any concerns.

- **Listen Carefully:** Take the time to fully understand the objection before responding. This shows that you value the customer's concerns and are committed to finding a solution.

2. **Reiterate the Value:**

- **Reinforce the Benefits:** When addressing an objection, reiterate the key benefits of your product or service. For example, if the customer is concerned about cost, emphasize the long-term savings or return on investment they can expect.
- **Provide Social Proof:** Use testimonials or case studies to demonstrate how other customers with similar concerns found success with your product. Seeing others overcome the same objections can reassure the customer.

Case Study: How HubSpot Masters the Close

HubSpot, a leading provider of inbound marketing and sales software, is known for its ability to close deals effectively. HubSpot's sales team uses a combination of assumptive closes, urgency, and personalized follow-up to convert leads into customers. By focusing on the customer's needs and providing ongoing value, HubSpot has built a reputation for closing deals with confidence and integrity.

Final Thoughts: Confidence Closes Deals

Closing a sale requires confidence, skill, and the ability to address last-minute objections. By mastering a variety of closing techniques, staying composed, and reinforcing the value of your product, you can close deals with confidence and achieve consistent sales success. Remember, the close is not just the end of the sales process—it's the beginning of a successful customer relationship.

Chapter 17:

Managing Stress in Sales: Strategies for Sustaining Success

Sales is often a high-pressure career. With targets to hit, clients to satisfy, and competition to outmaneuver, it's easy to see why stress is so common in the profession. However, managing stress effectively is crucial not only for maintaining personal well-being but also for sustaining long-term success in sales. This chapter will explore the sources of stress in sales and provide practical strategies for managing it, ensuring that you remain focused, motivated, and resilient.

Understanding the Sources of Stress in Sales

Sales can be stressful for many reasons. High expectations, constant performance evaluations, and the fear of failure are just a few of the pressures salespeople face daily. Additionally, the need to build relationships, manage rejection, and stay on top of ever-changing market conditions can contribute to a persistent sense of anxiety. Understanding these stressors is the first step toward managing them effectively.

Common Stressors in Sales

1. **Performance Pressure:**

- **Meeting Quotas:** Sales quotas are a primary source of stress. The pressure to meet or exceed targets can lead to anxiety, especially when goals are challenging or when the market is tough.
- **Constant Evaluation:** Sales professionals are often evaluated on their results, leading to a sense of being constantly under scrutiny. This can create a high level of stress, particularly if performance fluctuates.

2. **Client Interactions:**

- **Managing Expectations:** Clients can have high expectations, and the pressure to deliver on promises can be a significant source of stress. Handling difficult clients or situations where expectations are not met adds to the tension.
- **Handling Rejection:** Rejection is a part of sales, but it can be demoralizing. Constantly facing "no" can wear down even the most resilient salesperson, leading to self-doubt and stress.

3. **Market Dynamics:**

- **Competitive Environment:** Sales is inherently competitive, and the need to outperform competitors can be stressful. Keeping up with industry trends, competitor strategies, and market shifts requires constant vigilance.
- **Economic Uncertainty:** Economic downturns or shifts in market conditions can create uncertainty, making it difficult to predict outcomes and adding another layer of stress to the job.

Strategies for Managing Stress in Sales

1. **Time Management:**

- **Prioritize Tasks:** Effective time management is essential for reducing stress. Prioritize tasks based on urgency and importance, and focus on completing the most critical activities first. Breaking down large tasks into smaller, manageable steps can also reduce feelings of overwhelm.
- **Set Realistic Goals:** While it's important to aim high, setting realistic and achievable goals can help manage expectations and reduce stress. Consider breaking larger sales targets into smaller, more attainable milestones.

2. **Emotional Resilience:**
   - **Develop a Positive Mindset:** Cultivating a positive mindset can help you navigate the ups and downs of sales. Focus on the successes, no matter how small, and use setbacks as learning opportunities rather than reasons for self-criticism.
   - **Practice Mindfulness:** Mindfulness techniques, such as deep breathing exercises, meditation, and grounding techniques, can help reduce anxiety and improve focus. Incorporating mindfulness into your daily routine can help you stay calm and composed, even in high-pressure situations.

3. **Building a Support System:**
   - **Leverage Your Network:** Surround yourself with supportive colleagues, mentors, and friends who can offer advice, encouragement, and a listening ear. Sharing your challenges with others can help alleviate stress and provide new perspectives on difficult situations.
   - **Seek Professional Help:** If stress becomes overwhelming, consider seeking help from a professional, such as a coach or therapist. They can provide strategies for managing stress and improving mental well-being.

4. **Work-Life Balance:**
   - **Set Boundaries:** Maintaining a healthy work-life balance is crucial for managing stress. Set clear boundaries between work and personal life, and make time for activities that help you relax and recharge. Whether it's spending time with family, pursuing hobbies, or simply taking a break, ensuring you have downtime is essential for preventing burnout.
   - **Regular Physical Activity:** Exercise is a powerful stress reliever. Regular physical activity helps reduce stress hormones and increases the production of endorphins, the body's natural mood lifters. Incorporating exercise into

your routine can boost your energy levels, improve your mood, and help you manage stress more effectively.

Real-World Example: Overcoming Stress in Sales

Consider the experience of top sales professionals who have learned to manage stress effectively. Many credit their success to consistent routines, such as starting the day with meditation, setting clear goals, and maintaining a work-life balance. By managing stress, they are able to stay focused, maintain high energy levels, and continue to perform at their best, even in challenging conditions.

Final Thoughts: Stress Management as a Key to Sales Success

Stress is an inevitable part of a career in sales, but it doesn't have to be debilitating. By understanding the sources of stress and implementing effective management strategies, you can maintain your well-being, sustain your performance, and achieve long-term success. Remember, managing stress is not just about surviving in sales—it's about thriving. Prioritize your mental and physical health, and you'll find that success in sales follows naturally.

Chapter 18:
Handling Difficult Customers

Every salesperson encounters difficult customers at some point in their career. These are the customers who are hard to please, quick to anger, or seemingly impossible to satisfy. While dealing with difficult customers can be challenging, mastering this skill is crucial for maintaining your reputation, closing deals, and turning potential conflicts into opportunities for growth.

Understanding Difficult Customers

Difficult customers come in many forms. Some may be highly demanding, expecting instant results or special treatment. Others might be skeptical, doubting your product or service's value. There are also those who are simply unhappy with a previous experience, making them more critical of your current offering. Understanding the root cause of their behavior is the first step toward addressing their concerns effectively.

Strategies for Handling Difficult Customers

1. **Stay Calm and Composed:**

- **Control Your Emotions:** When faced with a difficult customer, it's essential to remain calm and composed. Reacting emotionally can escalate the situation, making it harder to resolve. Practice deep breathing or pause for a moment before responding to maintain control over your emotions.
- **Listen Actively:** Often, difficult customers just want to be heard. By actively listening to their concerns without interrupting, you show that you value their input. This can help de-escalate the situation and build trust.

2. **Empathy and Understanding:**
   - **Put Yourself in Their Shoes:** Try to understand the situation from the customer's perspective. Empathy can go a long way in making the customer feel understood and respected. Acknowledge their feelings and validate their concerns, even if you don't agree with them.
   - **Apologize When Necessary:** If the customer's dissatisfaction stems from a mistake on your part, offer a sincere apology. Taking responsibility for the issue shows integrity and can help rebuild trust.

3. **Problem-Solving with a Positive Attitude:**
   - **Focus on Solutions, Not Problems:** Once you understand the customer's concerns, shift the conversation towards finding a solution. Offer multiple options that address their needs and involve them in the decision-making process. This collaborative approach can turn a negative experience into a positive one.
   - **Stay Positive:** Maintain a positive attitude throughout the interaction. A positive mindset can help you remain resilient in the face of challenges and can influence the customer's attitude as well.

4. **Set Boundaries and Manage Expectations:**
   - **Know When to Say No:** While it's important to accommodate customers, there are times when you need to set boundaries. If a customer's demands are unreasonable, politely but firmly explain what you can and cannot do. It's better to manage expectations upfront than to promise something you can't deliver.
   - **Clear Communication:** Ensure that your communication is clear, concise, and free from ambiguity. This helps prevent misunderstandings and ensures that both you and the customer are on the same page.

Real-World Example: Turning a Difficult Situation Around

Consider a situation where a customer is unhappy with a product they purchased. Instead of becoming defensive, a skilled salesperson listens to the customer's concerns, apologizes for any inconvenience, and offers a free replacement or a discount on future purchases. By handling the situation with empathy and offering a solution, the salesperson not only resolves the issue but also retains the customer's loyalty.

Final Thoughts: Turning Challenges into Opportunities

Handling difficult customers is a skill that every successful salesperson must master. It's not just about resolving conflicts; it's about turning challenges into opportunities to strengthen customer relationships and build trust. By staying calm, empathetic, and solution-oriented, you can transform even the most difficult interactions into positive outcomes that benefit both you and your customers.

Chapter 19:

The Role of Creativity in Sales

In sales, creativity isn't just an added bonus—it's a necessity. The most successful salespeople are those who think outside the box, constantly innovate, and find new ways to connect with their customers. Creativity in sales means developing unique approaches to engage prospects, solve their problems, and ultimately close the deal. It's about breaking away from the standard, predictable sales tactics and instead offering something fresh and compelling.

Why Creativity Matters in Sales

Creativity is the engine that drives innovation and differentiation. In an overcrowded market, standing out is a challenge, and creativity provides the tools to make your product or service not just another option, but the only option in the minds of your customers. When you approach a prospect with a unique idea or an unconventional solution, you capture their attention and keep them interested. Creativity allows you to present your product or service in a way that resonates with the customer's specific needs, desires, and emotions.

Key Strategies for Harnessing Creativity in Sales

1. Personalization: Crafting Unique Experiences
   - **Tailoring the Message:** In today's market, a generic sales pitch is unlikely to succeed. Customers expect a personalized experience, and creativity is the key to delivering that. By tailoring your message to the specific needs and interests of each prospect, you make them feel valued and understood. This could involve using creative storytelling techniques to craft a narrative that resonates

- with their unique situation, or even designing custom solutions that directly address their pain points.
- **Engaging Storytelling:** Stories have a unique power to connect with people on an emotional level. By incorporating storytelling into your sales process, you can make your pitch more relatable and memorable. Share success stories of other clients, or create a narrative around how your product or service will transform the customer's business or life. The goal is to make the customer see themselves in the story you're telling.

2. **Innovative Problem-Solving: Outthink the Competition**
   - **Thinking Beyond the Obvious:** Creativity in problem-solving means going beyond the obvious solutions. When faced with a challenge or objection from a prospect, use creative problem-solving techniques to address their concerns in ways that your competitors haven't considered. This could involve offering an unexpected benefit, proposing a novel solution, or even reimagining how your product can be used in different scenarios. The ability to offer innovative solutions that others haven't thought of can be the key to winning over skeptical customers.
   - **Offering Multiple Options:** Instead of presenting a single solution, provide multiple options that address different aspects of the prospect's needs. This not only shows that you've thought deeply about their situation but also empowers them to choose the solution that feels most right for them. Giving customers choices can also increase their commitment to the decision they make.

3. **Leveraging New Tools and Technology: Stay Ahead of the Curve**
   - **Embracing Innovation:** Staying ahead of the curve in terms of tools and technology is crucial for maintaining a competitive edge. Whether it's using AI to analyze customer data, leveraging virtual reality for product demonstrations, or employing sophisticated CRM systems to manage relationships, being creative with technology can streamline your sales process and enhance your ability to close deals.
   - **Creative Content Marketing:** Use blogs, videos, and social media creatively to engage your audience. Share content that's not just promotional but also educational and entertaining. The goal is to position yourself as a thought leader in your industry, someone who offers value even before the sale is made. By providing content that is both informative and engaging, you build trust and credibility with your audience.

Real-World Example: Creativity in Action

Consider how Red Bull has used creativity to become a global powerhouse. Instead of simply marketing their energy drink, they created a brand around extreme sports, adventure, and pushing the limits. Their marketing campaigns, from sponsoring athletes to hosting their own events, are all rooted in creativity, making them more than just a beverage company—they're a lifestyle brand. This creative approach has not only differentiated Red Bull from its competitors but has also fostered a loyal customer base that resonates with the brand's identity.

Final Thoughts: Embrace Creativity to Elevate Your Sales

Creativity in sales isn't just a nice-to-have; it's a necessity. In a crowded marketplace, it's the creative salespeople who stand out, capture attention, and ultimately close more deals. By embracing creativity, you're not just selling a product—you're offering an experience, solving problems in unique ways, and building lasting relationships. So, start thinking creatively, and watch your sales soar.

Chapter 20:

Why Should the Customer Buy?

Every customer who considers your product is, consciously or subconsciously, asking the question: "Why should I buy this?" As a sales professional, your job is to answer that question clearly and convincingly. This chapter is about making your product's value so apparent that the customer can't help but see the benefits of making the purchase.

Understanding the Customer's Needs

Before you can answer why the customer should buy, you need to understand what they're looking for. Customers have specific needs, problems, and desires, and your product must be positioned as the best solution.

1. **Identify the Core Problem:**

    - **Listen First:** Engage with the customer to understand their primary concerns. What problem are they trying to solve? What are their pain points? The better you understand their needs, the better you can tailor your pitch.
    - **Align Your Product with Their Needs:** Once you know what the customer is looking for, clearly demonstrate how your product addresses these needs. Highlight the specific features and benefits that solve their problem.

2. **Make the Benefits Clear:**

    - **Focus on the Outcome:** Customers are more interested in the results they'll get from your product than the product itself. Whether it's saving time, increasing efficiency, or improving their quality of life, make sure the customer understands the tangible benefits.

- **Use Simple Language:** Avoid jargon and technical terms that might confuse the customer. Instead, use straightforward language that makes the benefits easy to grasp.

Building Trust and Credibility

Customers are more likely to buy from brands they trust. Establishing credibility is crucial in answering the question, "Why should I buy from you?"

1. **Prove Your Product Works:**

- **Share Testimonials and Case Studies:** Show the customer that others have benefited from your product. Real-world examples, testimonials, and case studies can provide the proof they need to trust your product.
- **Be Honest About Your Product:** Transparency builds trust. If there are limitations to your product, acknowledge them upfront and explain how you're addressing them. Customers appreciate honesty and are more likely to trust a brand that's upfront.

2. **Provide Guarantees:**

- **Offer Risk-Free Trials:** Let the customer try the product with minimal risk. A money-back guarantee or a free trial can reduce hesitation and make it easier for them to commit.
- **Showcase Your Support:** Let customers know that help is available if they need it. Whether it's customer service, a help center, or an easy return policy, knowing they're supported makes the decision to buy easier.

Differentiating Your Product

In a competitive market, standing out is essential. Your product needs to be the clear choice among all the options available to the customer.

1. **Highlight Your Unique Selling Proposition (USP):**
   - **What Makes You Different?** Clearly articulate what sets your product apart from the competition. Whether it's a unique feature, better value, or superior quality, make sure the customer knows why your product is the best choice.
   - **Simplify the Comparison:** Help the customer see why your product is the better option. Use comparisons or side-by-side charts to make it easy them to see the advantages.

2. **Create Urgency:**
   - **Limited-Time Offers:** Encourage the customer to act now by offering special deals or limited-time discounts. Creating a sense of urgency can push them to make a decision sooner rather than later.
   - **Scarcity Tactics:** Highlight the limited availability of your product to make it more desirable. When customers feel they might miss out, they're more likely to buy.

Final Thoughts: Answering the Question

When a customer asks, "Why should I buy?" they're giving you the opportunity to showcase the value of your product. By understanding their needs, building trust, and clearly differentiating your product, you can make a compelling case that not only answers their question but also motivates them to make the purchase. Remember, the goal is to make the decision to buy feel like the obvious and best choice.

Chapter 21:
Turn Customers into Your Sales Team

In the world of sales, one principle remains evergreen: word of mouth is powerful. But we're not talking about passive word of mouth. We're talking about putting your customers to work for you. The key? **Referrals**. If you're not leveraging referral marketing, you're leaving money on the table. Offering referral incentives doesn't just increase sales—it transforms satisfied customers into your most effective, unpaid sales force.

Why Referrals Are Your Hidden Sales Team

Referrals aren't just casual recommendations—they're direct, personal endorsements that carry weight. People trust their friends and colleagues more than any ad you could run. Referral marketing taps into this trust, creating a direct line to new customers who are already primed to buy. It's social proof on steroids.

Think about it: A new customer who's referred by a friend is almost guaranteed to engage with your product or service, and here's why:

- **Higher Trust:** When a friend says, "I love this product," they've already done the convincing for you.
- **Faster Conversions:** Referred customers often skip the research phase because they trust their friend's recommendation. That means quicker decisions and faster sales.
- **Repeat Business:** Satisfied referrals are more likely to become repeat customers and refer others, creating a powerful loop of continuous growth.

How to Craft a Referral Program That Actually Works

1. Offer Irresistible Rewards:

- **Mutual Win-Win:** The best referral programs reward both the referrer and the referred. Give your existing customer something they'll actually value—whether it's cash, a discount, or a free product. The reward for the new customer can be a juicy first-time discount or a bonus service.
- **Make It Worth Their Time:** People won't refer their friends for a 5% discount. Offer something significant that makes it worth their while. A flat $20 off or a free upgrade will make customers eager to send business your way.

2. Simplify the Referral Process:

- **One Click, One Code:** Make it stupidly easy for your customers to refer. Provide a referral link or code they can send via email or social media. The easier it is, the more likely they are to share.
- **Mobile-Friendly:** Make sure the referral process works seamlessly on mobile devices. Most customers will refer directly from their phones, so a mobile-optimized referral program is a must.

3. Strike While the Iron's Hot:

- **Perfect Timing:** The best time to ask for a referral? Right after a customer has had a positive experience with your product or service. Follow up with an email saying, "Loved your purchase? Share it with a friend and get $20 off your next order!"
- **Urgency + Reward:** Create urgency with limited-time referral offers. For example, offer an extra bonus if they refer within the first 30 days of their purchase. This encourages quick action.

4. **Gamify It:**
   - **Tiered Rewards:** Think bigger—turn your referral program into a game. Offer tiered rewards for multiple referrals. Maybe the first gets them a 10% discount, but three referrals unlock a free product, and five get them a VIP status with exclusive perks. People love a challenge and will keep referring if there's a bigger prize at the end.
   - **Leaderboard:** If your product or service is community-based, consider a referral leaderboard where top referrers get public recognition and even bigger rewards.

Real-World Domination: Uber's Referral Machine

Uber didn't just disrupt the taxi industry—they obliterated it. One of their secret weapons? An aggressive referral program. Uber offered free rides to both the referrer and the new user. The simplicity and high value of the offer turned every rider into a brand ambassador. This strategy propelled Uber from a small startup to a global powerhouse in record time.

From Customers to Ambassadors

When you turn your customers into ambassadors, you're no longer the only one selling. Your customers become your sales force, and that's a game-changer. Here's what that looks like in practice:

Lower Acquisition Costs: With a solid referral program, you're acquiring new customers at a fraction of the cost of traditional advertising.
- **Higher Quality Leads:** Referrals are warm leads—these customers trust you before they even hear your pitch.
- **Customer Loyalty:** Customers who refer others feel a personal connection to your brand. The more they refer, the more loyal they become.

Final Thoughts: Unleash the Referral Engine

Stop spending insane amounts of money on traditional advertising. Your greatest sales team is already in front of you: your happy customers. All you have to do is give them a reason to talk and a reward for doing it. Referrals are not just an afterthought—they're a sales strategy that turns satisfied buyers into loyal advocates and, ultimately, the most powerful sales machines in your business arsenal.

Chapter 22:

Adapting to Change: Staying Agile in Sales

In today's fast-paced market, the ability to adapt is not just an advantage—it's a necessity. The sales landscape is constantly evolving, driven by changes in technology, customer behavior, and market conditions. Sales professionals who can stay agile, quickly pivot, and adapt to these changes are the ones who thrive. This chapter explores the importance of agility in sales and provides strategies for staying flexible and responsive in a dynamic environment.

Why Agility is Crucial in Sales

Sales agility refers to the ability to quickly adjust strategies, tactics, and approaches in response to changes. Whether it's a sudden shift in customer needs, a new competitor entering the market, or an economic downturn, being agile allows you to remain effective and competitive. In contrast, rigid sales approaches often lead to missed opportunities and declining performance.

Key Components of Sales Agility

1. **Market Awareness:**
   - **Staying Informed:** To stay agile, you must be aware of what's happening in your market. This includes tracking industry trends, monitoring competitor activities, and staying informed about changes in customer preferences. The more aware you are, the quicker you can respond to changes.

- **Anticipating Shifts:** Agility is not just about reacting to change but anticipating it. By keeping a close eye on market signals, you can identify potential shifts before they happen and prepare your strategy accordingly.

2. **Flexible Strategies:**
- **Dynamic Sales Approaches:** Adopt sales strategies that are flexible and adaptable. This might include having multiple sales pitches ready to go, each tailored to different customer segments or scenarios. The key is to avoid a one-size-fits-all approach.
- **Quick Iteration:** Agility involves the ability to quickly test and iterate on sales strategies. If something isn't working, don't be afraid to change course. Regularly assess the effectiveness of your tactics and be willing to make adjustments on the fly.

3. **Customer-Centric Adaptation:**
- **Listening to Feedback:** Customer feedback is a valuable resource for staying agile. Regularly solicit feedback from your customers to understand their evolving needs and preferences. Use this information to adapt your sales approach and improve your offerings.
- **Personalized Engagement:** Agility in sales often means personalizing your approach for each customer. Tailor your communication, offers, and follow-ups based on the unique circumstances of each prospect.

Strategies for Staying Agile

1. **Embrace Technology:**
- **Leverage Sales Tools:** Modern sales tools can enhance your ability to stay agile. CRM systems, analytics platforms, and automation tools allow you to quickly gather data, analyze

results, and adjust your approach. Invest in technology that supports flexibility and real-time decision-making.
- **Virtual Sales:** The shift to digital sales channels has made agility even more critical. Virtual sales techniques, such as video conferencing and online demos, enable you to reach customers quickly and adapt to their availability and preferences.

2. **Agile Sales Training:**

- **Continuous Learning:** Encourage a culture of continuous learning within your sales team. Regular training sessions on new tools, techniques, and market trends will keep your team adaptable and ready to tackle new challenges.
- **Role-Playing and Simulation:** Use role-playing exercises and sales simulations to practice agility. By simulating different scenarios, your team can develop the skills needed to respond effectively to various customer situations.

3. **Resilience and Mindset:**

- **Adopting a Growth Mindset:** Agility in sales is closely tied to having a growth mindset. Embrace challenges as opportunities to learn and improve. Resilience in the face of setbacks is essential for maintaining agility.
- **Stress Management:** Agility also involves managing stress and staying calm under pressure. Techniques such as mindfulness, exercise, and time management can help you maintain composure and make clear-headed decisions in rapidly changing situations.

Real-World Example: Agility in Action

Consider how Netflix adapted its business model in response to changing consumer preferences. Originally a DVD rental service, Netflix quickly shifted to a streaming model as internet speeds improved and customer demand for instant access to content grew. By staying agile and adapting to technological advancements and market demands, Netflix became a dominant player in the entertainment industry.

Final Thoughts: Embrace Agility to Stay Ahead

In the ever-changing world of sales, agility is your competitive advantage. By staying informed, embracing flexibility, and continuously adapting to new challenges, you can maintain your edge in the market. Remember, the ability to pivot quickly and effectively can make the difference between surviving and thriving in sales. Stay agile, and you'll be prepared for whatever comes your way.

Chapter 23:

The Psychology of Money: Changing Your Mindset

Your mindset towards money plays a critical role in how you manage your finances, make investment decisions, and ultimately build wealth. This chapter explores the psychology of money and how changing your mindset can lead to better financial decisions and a more prosperous life.

The Role of Money Mindset

Your money mindset is the set of beliefs and attitudes you hold about money, which influences your financial behaviors and decisions. A positive money mindset can lead to smart financial choices, while a negative mindset can result in poor financial habits and missed opportunities.

Common Money Mindsets and Their Impact

1. **Scarcity Mindset:**

- **The Fear of Never Having Enough:** A scarcity mindset is characterized by the fear of never having enough money, leading to hoarding, excessive frugality, or anxiety around spending. This mindset can prevent you from taking calculated risks or investing in opportunities that could lead to financial growth.
- **Breaking Free:** To overcome a scarcity mindset, focus on abundance. Shift your thinking from "I can't afford this" to "How can I afford this?" Embrace the idea that opportunities for wealth are abundant and that with the right strategies, you can create financial security.

2. **Growth Mindset:**
   - **Belief in Financial Growth:** A growth mindset in finance is the belief that you can improve your financial situation through learning, effort, and perseverance. People with a growth mindset are more likely to seek out financial education, invest in themselves, and take strategic risks.
   - **Cultivating a Growth Mindset:** To cultivate a growth mindset, focus on learning and self-improvement. Set financial goals, track your progress, and celebrate small wins. Understand that setbacks are part of the journey and use them as learning experiences to make better decisions in the future.

3. **Fixed Mindset:**
   - **Belief That Your Financial Situation is Static:** A fixed mindset assumes that your financial situation is unchangeable. This can lead to complacency or a lack of motivation to improve your financial health. For example, believing that you're "just bad with money" can prevent you from seeking ways to improve.
   - **Shifting to a Growth Mindset:** Challenge the belief that your financial situation is static. Recognize that everyone has the potential to improve their financial literacy and make better decisions. Seek out resources, mentors, and education to help you grow.

Changing Your Money Mindset

1. **Set Clear Financial Goals:**
   - **Define What You Want:** Start by setting clear, achievable financial goals. Whether it's saving for a down payment on a house, paying off debt, or building an emergency fund, having specific goals gives you direction and motivation.

- **Break Goals into Actionable Steps:** Break your goals down into smaller, actionable steps. For example, if your goal is to save $10,000, set a monthly savings target and automate your savings to ensure consistency.

2. **Practice Gratitude and Abundance:**

- **Shift Focus to What You Have:** Practicing gratitude helps shift your focus from what you lack to what you have. This shift in perspective can reduce feelings of scarcity and increase your sense of financial well-being.
- **Celebrate Financial Wins:** No matter how small, celebrate your financial successes. Whether it's paying off a credit card or reaching a savings milestone, acknowledging your progress reinforces a positive money mindset.

3. **Educate Yourself About Money:**

- **Invest in Financial Education:** Financial literacy is key to making informed decisions and building wealth. Invest in your financial education by reading books, attending workshops, or taking online courses on money management, investing, and wealth building.
- **Surround Yourself with Like-Minded Individuals:** Join financial communities or groups where you can learn from others, share experiences, and stay motivated. Being part of a community that values financial growth can reinforce positive behaviors and mindsets.

Case Study: How a Growth Mindset Transformed an Investor

Consider the story of an investor who started with minimal knowledge of the stock market but had a strong growth mindset. By dedicating time to learning about investments, seeking advice from experienced investors, and consistently applying what they learned, they were able to grow their portfolio significantly over time. Their willingness to learn and adapt allowed them to overcome initial setbacks and achieve long-term financial success.

Final Thoughts: Mindset is the Foundation of Wealth

Your money mindset is the foundation upon which your financial success is built. By shifting from a scarcity or fixed mindset to one of growth and abundance, you can make better financial decisions, take advantage of opportunities, and build lasting wealth. Remember, wealth is not just about the money you earn—it's about the mindset you cultivate and the choices you make.

Chapter 24:

Cash Flow Power: Control the Money, Control the Game

Cash flow is the lifeblood of your business, and controlling it effectively can mean the difference between success and failure. This chapter focuses on strategies to master cash flow management, ensuring your business remains financially healthy and capable of seizing growth opportunities.

Why Cash Flow Matters

Cash flow refers to the movement of money in and out of your business. Positive cash flow means you have more money coming in than going out, which is crucial for paying bills, reinvesting in your business, and covering unexpected expenses. Negative cash flow, on the other hand, can lead to financial strain and potentially jeopardize your business's future.

Key Strategies for Cash Flow Management

1. **Monitor Cash Flow Regularly:**

- **Track Inflows and Outflows:** Regularly monitor your cash flow to keep a close eye on the money coming in and going out of your business. Use cash flow statements and forecasting tools to track trends and anticipate future cash needs.
- **Set Alerts for Critical Changes:** Set up alerts in your accounting software to notify you of significant changes in cash flow, such as a sudden drop in revenue or an unexpected expense. This allows you to take action quickly and prevent small issues from escalating.

2. **Optimize Receivables:**
   - **Speed Up Payments:** Encourage customers to pay promptly by offering incentives for early payments, such as discounts or bonuses. Consider using automated invoicing and payment reminders to reduce delays and improve cash flow.
   - **Reduce Payment Terms:** If possible, reduce your payment terms to encourage faster payments. For example, switch from net 60 to net 30 payment terms to shorten the time between invoicing and receiving payment.

3. **Manage Payables Wisely:**
   - **Negotiate Favorable Terms:** Negotiate payment terms with suppliers that allow you to keep cash in your business for longer. For example, extend payment terms or take advantage of early payment discounts to optimize cash flow.
   - **Prioritize Payments:** If cash flow is tight, prioritize payments based on their importance to your business's operations. Pay essential suppliers and bills first, while negotiating extensions for less critical expenses.

4. **Build a Cash Reserve:**
   - **Create a Safety Net:** Establish a cash reserve to cover unexpected expenses or slow periods. This reserve acts as a financial buffer, allowing you to weather challenges without disrupting your operations.
   - **Plan for Seasonality:** If your business experiences seasonal fluctuations in revenue, plan your cash flow accordingly. Save excess cash during peak periods to cover expenses during slower months.

Maximizing Cash Flow for Growth

Once you've established strong cash flow management practices, the next step is to use your positive cash flow to fuel business growth.

1. **Reinvest in Your Business:**
   - **Fund Growth Initiatives:** Use your cash flow to fund growth initiatives, such as expanding your product line, increasing marketing efforts, or entering new markets. Reinvesting profits into your business helps you build momentum and achieve long-term success.
   - **Upgrade Equipment and Technology:** Invest in new equipment, technology, or software that can enhance productivity and efficiency. This not only improves your operations but also positions your business for future growth.

2. **Expand Your Cash Flow Streams:**
   - **Diversify Revenue Streams:** Explore opportunities to diversify your revenue streams, such as introducing new products or services, targeting different customer segments, or expanding into new geographic areas. Diversification reduces risk and increases your business's resilience.
   - **Leverage Financing Options:** If you need additional capital to fund growth, consider financing options such as business loans, lines of credit, or investor funding. Ensure that any financing you secure aligns with your cash flow needs and repayment capacity.

Case Study: How Amazon Manages Cash Flow for Growth

Amazon is a prime example of a company that has mastered cash flow management to fuel rapid growth. By optimizing its supply chain, negotiating favorable payment terms with suppliers, and reinvesting profits into new ventures, Amazon has consistently maintained positive cash flow. This financial discipline has enabled Amazon to expand its operations, acquire new businesses, and become one of the most valuable companies in the world.

Final Thoughts: Master Your Cash, Master Your Future

Effective cash control is essential for the survival and growth of your business. By monitoring cash flow, optimizing receivables and payables, and maintaining a cash reserve, you can ensure financial stability and position your business for long-term success. Remember, cash is king, and mastering your money is the key to building a sustainable and prosperous future for your business.

Chapter 25:

Brand Like a Boss: Rule Your Market

In today's competitive market, building a strong personal or business brand is essential for standing out and achieving success. Your brand is more than just a logo or a tagline—it's the reputation and identity that you build over time. This chapter explores strategies for building a powerful brand that dominates your market and resonates with your target audience.

The Importance of Branding

A strong brand sets you apart from competitors, builds trust with your audience, and creates loyalty among customers. Whether you're an entrepreneur, a small business owner, or a professional, branding is a critical component of your long-term success.

Key Elements of a Strong Brand

1. Clarity of Purpose:

- **Define Your Brand's Mission:** Your brand's purpose is the foundation of its identity. Clearly define what your brand stands for, what it aims to achieve, and why it exists. A strong purpose resonates with customers and differentiates you from competitors.
- **Align Your Brand with Customer Values:** Ensure that your brand's mission aligns with the values and needs of your target audience. When customers see that your brand shares their values, they are more likely to develop a strong connection with it.

2. **Consistency Across Channels:**
   - **Maintain a Cohesive Brand Image:** Consistency is key to building a recognizable brand. Ensure that your messaging, visuals, and tone are consistent across all channels, from your website and social media to your packaging and customer service.
   - **Develop Brand Guidelines:** Create brand guidelines that outline your brand's visual identity, tone of voice, and key messaging. These guidelines ensure that everyone involved in your brand's communication maintains consistency.

3. **Authenticity and Transparency:**
   - **Be Genuine:** Authenticity builds trust. Be genuine in your communications and actions, and avoid making promises that you can't keep. Customers value honesty and are more likely to remain loyal to brands that are transparent.
   - **Share Your Story:** Share the story behind your brand—how it started, the challenges you've overcome, and the values that drive you. A compelling brand story creates an emotional connection with your audience.

4. **Customer-Centric Approach:**
   - **Focus on Customer Experience:** Your brand is defined by how customers perceive it, so prioritize delivering an exceptional customer experience. From the first interaction to post-purchase support, ensure that every touchpoint reinforces your brand's values and promises.
   - **Engage with Your Audience:** Actively engage with your audience through social media, email marketing, and other channels. Listen to their feedback, respond to their inquiries, and involve them in your brand's journey. Engaged customers are more likely to become loyal advocates.

Building and Maintaining Brand Authority

1. **Position Yourself as an Expert:**

- **Share Valuable Content:** Establish your brand as an authority in your industry by sharing valuable content that educates, informs, and inspires your audience. This could include blog posts, webinars, videos, or podcasts that showcase your expertise.
- **Leverage Thought Leadership:** Contribute to industry discussions, speak at events, and collaborate with influencers or experts in your field. Thought leadership enhances your brand's credibility and visibility.

2. **Create a Community Around Your Brand:**

- **Foster a Sense of Belonging:** Build a community of loyal customers and fans who share your brand's values and mission. Create spaces, such as social media groups or forums, where they can connect with each other and with your brand.
- **Encourage User-Generated Content:** Encourage your community to share their experiences with your brand through photos, reviews, and testimonials. Featuring user-generated content on your platforms reinforces the sense of community and strengthens brand loyalty.

3. **Innovate and Evolve:**

- **Stay Relevant:** The market is constantly changing, and your brand needs to evolve to stay relevant. Continuously innovate your products, services, and marketing strategies to meet the changing needs of your audience.
- **Monitor Brand Perception:** Regularly monitor how your brand is perceived by your audience. Use surveys, social listening tools, and customer feedback to gauge sentiment and make adjustments as needed.

Case Study: How Nike Built an Iconic Brand

Nike is one of the most iconic brands in the world, known for its powerful branding and ability to connect with customers on an emotional level. Through consistent messaging, authentic storytelling, and a customer-centric approach, Nike has built a brand that not only dominates the athletic market but also resonates with a global audience. Nike's "Just Do It" campaign, for example, is a masterclass in branding, conveying a message of empowerment that transcends sports and inspires people from all walks of life.

Final Thoughts: Brand Like a Boss

Building a strong brand is essential for long-term success in today's competitive market. By focusing on clarity of purpose, consistency, authenticity, and customer-centricity, you can create a brand that not only stands out but also rules your market. Remember, branding is not just about visuals—it's about the experience and emotional connection you create with your audience. When done right, your brand becomes more than just a business; it becomes a movement that inspires and attracts loyal followers.

Chapter 26:

Bank on Social Proof: Transform Testimonials into Cash

Social proof is a powerful psychological phenomenon that can significantly influence buying decisions. When potential customers see others endorsing your product or service, they're more likely to trust your brand and make a purchase. This chapter explores how to leverage social proof, such as testimonials, reviews, and endorsements, to boost your sales and build credibility.

The Psychology Behind Social Proof

Social proof works because humans are inherently social creatures. We tend to follow the actions of others, especially when we're unsure about what to do. When people see others using and enjoying a product, they assume it must be good. This herd mentality is why testimonials and reviews can be so persuasive—they provide evidence that your product or service delivers on its promises.

Types of Social Proof

1. **Testimonials:**

- **Real Voices, Real Impact:** Testimonials from satisfied customers can be incredibly influential. They provide real-world evidence of your product's benefits and help potential customers visualize the positive outcomes they could experience.
- **Video Testimonials:** Video testimonials can be even more impactful than written ones. Seeing and hearing a real person talk about their positive experience with your

product can create a stronger emotional connection and build trust more quickly.

2. **Reviews:**

- **Crowd Wisdom:** Online reviews are a form of social proof that many customers rely on before making a purchase. Encourage satisfied customers to leave reviews on platforms like Google, Yelp, or industry-specific sites.
- **Highlighting Positive Reviews:** Feature your best reviews prominently on your website and in your marketing materials. Positive reviews not only build credibility but also address potential customers' concerns before they become objections.

3. **Case Studies:**

- **In-Depth Success Stories:** Case studies provide a detailed account of how your product or service has helped a specific customer achieve their goals. They're particularly effective in B2B sales, where decision-makers need proof that your solution can deliver measurable results.
- **Data-Driven Results:** Include statistics, metrics, and clear outcomes in your case studies to make them more compelling. Numbers can provide concrete evidence that reinforces the narrative of success.

4. **Influencer Endorsements:**

- **Leveraging Authority:** Influencers have built-in audiences that trust their recommendations. Partnering with influencers in your industry can amplify your brand's reach and credibility.
- **Authentic Promotion:** Choose influencers whose values align with your brand. Authentic endorsements resonate more with audiences and are more likely to result in conversions.

How to Use Social Proof to Drive Sales

1. **Integrate Social Proof Throughout the Customer Journey:**

- **Website:** Place testimonials, reviews, and case studies on key pages like your homepage, product pages, and checkout page. This reinforces trust at every stage of the buyer's journey.
- **Email Marketing:** Include customer testimonials and positive reviews in your email campaigns to build credibility and encourage action.
- **Social Media:** Share user-generated content, testimonials, and influencer endorsements on your social media channels. This not only boosts engagement but also provides potential customers with the reassurance they need to move forward.

2. **Encourage User-Generated Content:**

- **Incentivize Sharing:** Encourage customers to share their experiences with your product on social media by offering incentives like discounts, giveaways, or features on your channels.
- **Create a Community:** Build a community around your brand where customers can share their stories, interact with each other, and provide valuable social proof that reinforces your brand's credibility.

3. **Respond to Reviews:**

- **Engage and Show Appreciation:** Respond to both positive and negative reviews. Thank customers for their feedback and address any concerns raised in negative reviews. This shows that you value customer input and are committed to continuous improvement.

Case Study: How Glossier Used Social Proof to Build a Beauty Empire

Glossier, a beauty brand known for its minimalist products, has built its success largely on social proof. The brand encourages customers to share their experiences on social media, often featuring user-generated content on its own platforms. By leveraging the power of social proof, Glossier has created a community-driven brand that resonates deeply with its audience, resulting in a loyal customer base and impressive sales growth.

Final Thoughts: Social Proof as a Sales Tool

Social proof isn't just a nice-to-have; it's a powerful tool that can significantly impact your sales. By strategically incorporating testimonials, reviews, case studies, and influencer endorsements into your marketing efforts, you can build trust, overcome objections, and drive conversions. Remember, in the world of sales, what others say about you often carries more weight than what you say about yourself.

Chapter 27:
Road Map to Wealth: Financial Planning for Entrepreneurs

Financial planning is the cornerstone of business success. As an entrepreneur, having a clear financial plan allows you to manage your resources effectively, make informed decisions, and achieve your long-term goals. This chapter provides a comprehensive road map to wealth, focusing on key financial planning strategies tailored for entrepreneurs.

The Importance of Financial Planning

Financial planning helps you understand your current financial position, set realistic goals, and develop strategies to achieve those goals. Without a solid financial plan, you risk running into cash flow problems, overspending, or missing out on growth opportunities.

Key Components of a Financial Plan

1. **Budgeting and Forecasting:**
   - **Create a Detailed Budget:** Start by creating a detailed budget that outlines your income, expenses, and savings. Include both fixed and variable costs, and review your budget regularly to ensure you're staying on track.
   - **Forecast Future Financial Needs:** Use forecasting to predict your future financial needs based on your business's growth projections. This helps you plan for investments, hiring, and other expenses that will support your growth.

2. **Cash Flow Management:**
   - **Monitor Cash Flow:** Regularly track your cash flow to ensure that your business has enough liquidity to cover its

expenses. Use cash flow statements and projections to anticipate periods of high or low cash flow and plan accordingly.
- **Improve Cash Flow:** Look for ways to improve cash flow, such as speeding up receivables, negotiating better payment terms with suppliers, or reducing unnecessary expenses.

3. **Debt Management:**

- **Manage Existing Debt:** If your business has debt, create a plan to manage and pay it off. Focus on paying down high-interest debt first to reduce your overall interest expenses.
- **Use Debt Strategically:** While debt can be a useful tool for financing growth, it's important to use it strategically. Only take on debt that you can manage and that will contribute to your long-term financial goals.

4. **Investment Strategies:**

- **Reinvest in Your Business:** Consider reinvesting a portion of your profits back into your business to fund growth initiatives, such as expanding your product line, increasing marketing efforts, or entering new markets.
- **Diversify Investments:** In addition to reinvesting in your business, consider diversifying your investments to reduce risk and build wealth. This could include investing in stocks, bonds, real estate, or other assets.

5. **Risk Management:**

- **Protect Your Business:** Implement risk management strategies to protect your business from financial loss. This could include purchasing insurance, setting aside a cash reserve, or diversifying your revenue streams.
- **Plan for the Unexpected:** Prepare for unexpected events, such as economic downturns or emergencies, by having a

contingency plan in place. This ensures that your business can continue to operate even in challenging circumstances.

Setting Financial Goals

1. **Short-Term Goals:**

- **Focus on Immediate Needs:** Short-term financial goals typically cover the next 1-3 years and focus on immediate needs, such as building an emergency fund, paying off debt, or saving for a specific investment.
- **Set Realistic Milestones:** Break down your short-term goals into achievable milestones and track your progress regularly. This helps you stay motivated and ensures that you're making steady progress toward your goals.

2. **Long-Term Goals:**

- **Plan for the Future:** Long-term financial goals are typically 5-10 years or more and focus on future growth, retirement planning, or major investments. Setting long-term goals helps you stay focused on the bigger picture and make decisions that align with your vision for the future.
- **Adjust as Needed:** As your business grows and evolves, your financial goals may change. Regularly review and adjust your long-term goals to ensure they remain relevant and achievable.

Case Study: How a Financial Plan Saved a Startup

Consider the story of a startup that struggled with cash flow problems during its early stages. By developing a detailed financial plan, the founders were able to identify areas where they were overspending, implement cost-saving measures, and secure additional funding. This financial discipline not only helped the startup survive its early challenges but also positioned it for long-term growth and success.

Final Thoughts: The Road Map to Wealth

Financial planning is essential for any entrepreneur who wants to build a successful and sustainable business. By creating a comprehensive financial plan that includes budgeting, cash flow management, debt management, investment strategies, and risk management, you can set your business on the path to long-term wealth and financial security. Remember, the road to wealth is not just about making money—it's about making smart financial decisions that support your goals and ensure your business thrives.

Chapter 28:

The Power of Consistency: Building Habits for Long-Term Success

Success in sales, business, and personal growth doesn't come from sporadic efforts; it comes from consistency. Whether it's consistently delivering value to customers, consistently learning and adapting, or consistently putting in the effort day after day, the power of consistency cannot be overstated.

Why Consistency Matters

Consistency builds trust, creates momentum, and leads to mastery. When you show up every day and put in the work, you build a reputation as someone who can be relied upon. This applies not just to your customers, but also to your colleagues, partners, and even yourself.

Building Consistent Habits

1. **Start with Small, Daily Actions:**

- **The Power of Small Wins:** Big successes are often the result of small, consistent actions over time. Whether it's making a few sales calls every day, setting aside time for personal development, or maintaining regular customer follow-ups, these small actions add up to significant results.
- **Establish Routine:** Develop a daily routine that includes your most important tasks. This routine becomes the foundation of your consistency. Whether it's the first thing in the morning or during a specific time block, make sure these tasks are non-negotiable.

2. **Focus on Progress, Not Perfection:**
   - **Embrace Imperfection:** Consistency doesn't mean being perfect every time. It's about showing up and making progress, even if it's not perfect. Perfectionism can be paralyzing, but consistent action leads to improvement and mastery over time.
   - **Track Your Progress:** Keep track of your efforts and celebrate small victories. Whether it's a journal, an app, or a simple checklist, tracking your progress helps maintain momentum and keeps you motivated.

3. **Overcoming Obstacles to Consistency:**
   - **Identify Your Roadblocks:** What's preventing you from being consistent? Is it time management, lack of motivation, or external distractions? Identifying these obstacles allows you to address them head-on.
   - **Stay Accountable:** Whether it's through a mentor, a peer group, or self-monitoring, accountability is crucial for maintaining consistency. Regular check-ins or progress reviews help keep you on track and committed to your goals.

Examples of Consistency in Action

Consider the example of Dwayne "The Rock" Johnson, who is known for his relentless work ethic. Whether it's his fitness routine, his acting career, or his business ventures, Johnson's consistency has been a key factor in his success. He often talks about the importance of showing up every day, putting in the work, and staying committed to the process, no matter how tough it gets.

Final Thoughts: Consistency is Key

In the journey to becoming a sales god, a business titan, or achieving personal growth, consistency is your greatest ally. It's not about grand gestures or sporadic efforts; it's about the daily grind, the small actions, and the unwavering commitment to your goals. When you embrace the power of consistency, you build habits that lead to long-term success and mastery in your field.

Chapter 29:

The Power of Mindset: Cultivating a Winning Mentality

In the journey of personal and financial growth, your mindset is your greatest asset. The way you think about challenges, opportunities, and your own potential shapes every aspect of your life. A winning mentality isn't about being born with certain traits; it's about cultivating habits and beliefs that drive you towards success.

Why Mindset Matters

Your mindset is the lens through which you view the world. It influences your actions, your reactions, and ultimately, your outcomes. By developing a positive, growth-oriented mindset, you empower yourself to take on challenges, learn from failures, and continuously strive for better results.

Cultivating a Winning Mentality

1. **Embrace the Growth Mindset:**

- **Believe in Your Ability to Improve:** The growth mindset is the belief that your abilities and intelligence can be developed with effort, learning, and persistence. Embracing this mindset means seeing challenges as opportunities to grow rather than as threats to your self-worth.
- **Learn from Failures:** Instead of seeing failures as final, view them as stepping stones to success. Every failure is an opportunity to learn and grow. By analyzing what went wrong, you can make adjustments and improve your chances of success in the future.

2. **Stay Resilient in the Face of Adversity:**
   - **Build Mental Toughness:** Life is full of setbacks, but it's how you respond to them that defines your success. Mental toughness is about staying focused, determined, and positive, even when things get tough. It's about bouncing back from difficulties with even more resolve.
   - **Focus on What You Can Control:** In any situation, there are factors you can control and factors you can't. By focusing on what you can control—your attitude, your actions, and your efforts—you empower yourself to make the best of any situation.

3. **Practice Gratitude and Positivity:**
   - **Shift Your Perspective:** Practicing gratitude helps you focus on what's going right in your life, rather than what's going wrong. This shift in perspective can boost your mood, increase your resilience, and improve your overall outlook on life.
   - **Surround Yourself with Positivity:** The people you spend time with and the content you consume have a big impact on your mindset. Surround yourself with positive influences—friends who encourage you, mentors who inspire you, and content that uplifts you.

Real-Life Example: The Power of a Winning Mindset

Consider the story of J.K. Rowling, the author of the Harry Potter series. Before achieving success, she faced numerous rejections from publishers, financial difficulties, and personal challenges. However, her belief in her story and her resilience in the face of adversity eventually led her to become one of the most successful authors of all time. Rowling's journey is a testament to the power of a winning mindset—believing in yourself, learning from setbacks, and never giving up.

Final Thoughts: Mindset is Everything

Your mindset is the foundation of your success. By cultivating a winning mentality, you equip yourself with the tools to navigate life's challenges, seize opportunities, and achieve your goals. Remember, it's not about where you start; it's about the mindset you develop along the way. Embrace the power of mindset, and watch as it transforms your life.

Chapter 30:

Investing in Yourself: The Best Investment You'll Ever Make

When it comes to building wealth and achieving success, the most important investment you can make is in yourself. Unlike material investments that can fluctuate in value, the skills, knowledge, and experiences you gain will continue to pay dividends throughout your life. Investing in yourself is about maximizing your potential, opening new doors, and ultimately increasing your ability to generate income and achieve your goals.

Why Investing in Yourself Matters

Investing in yourself boosts your confidence, enhances your skillset, and expands your opportunities. Whether it's through education, personal development, or health and wellness, the time and resources you put into self-improvement have a direct impact on your success and overall quality of life.

Ways to Invest in Yourself

1. **Education and Skill Development:**

- **Pursue Further Education:** Whether it's a degree, certification, or specialized training, continuing your education can open doors to new career opportunities and increase your earning potential. Focus on areas that are in demand or that align with your passions and goals.
- **Learn New Skills:** The job market is constantly evolving, and the ability to adapt is crucial. Identify skills that are relevant to your industry and invest time in mastering them. This could be anything from learning a new language to developing technical skills like coding or digital marketing.

2. **Health and Wellness:**
   - **Prioritize Physical Health:** Your physical well-being directly impacts your productivity and mental clarity. Invest in a healthy lifestyle by maintaining a balanced diet, exercising regularly, and getting enough sleep. The benefits of good health extend beyond the physical—it also boosts your mood, energy levels, and resilience.
   - **Focus on Mental Health:** Mental well-being is just as important as physical health. Practice stress management techniques like meditation, mindfulness, or therapy. Taking care of your mental health helps you stay focused, motivated, and capable of handling challenges.

3. **Personal Growth and Development:**
   - **Set Personal Goals:** Personal growth is about continuously challenging yourself to be better. Set clear, achievable goals for personal development, whether it's improving your communication skills, building better relationships, or developing a positive mindset.
   - **Cultivate a Growth Mindset:** Embrace the belief that your abilities can be developed through effort and learning. This mindset encourages you to take on challenges, learn from failures, and keep pushing forward.

Real-Life Example: The Impact of Self-Investment

Consider the story of Oprah Winfrey. Despite a challenging upbringing, Oprah invested in herself through education, self-improvement, and personal growth. Her commitment to learning and development transformed her from a local news anchor to one of the most influential media moguls in the world. Oprah's journey is a testament to the power of self-investment—showing that when you invest in yourself, the possibilities are endless.

Final Thoughts: You Are Your Greatest Asset

Investing in yourself is the foundation of success. It's about recognizing your own potential and taking deliberate steps to nurture and develop it. Whether through education, health, or personal growth, the time and resources you invest in yourself will yield returns far greater than any other investment you can make. Remember, you are your greatest asset—invest in yourself wisely.

Chapter 31:

Passive Income Strategies: Building Wealth While You Sleep

Passive income is the key to financial freedom. Unlike active income, which requires continuous effort to earn, passive income allows you to generate wealth with minimal ongoing effort. By building multiple streams of passive income, you can create financial security, reduce dependence on a single source of income, and achieve your financial goals more quickly.

Understanding Passive Income

Passive income is money earned with little to no effort after the initial setup. It's about putting in the work upfront to create a system that continues to generate income on its own. Examples include rental income, dividends from investments, royalties from creative work, or earnings from a business that you don't actively manage.

Strategies for Building Passive Income

1. **Real Estate Investments:**

- **Rental Properties:** Investing in rental properties is one of the most popular ways to generate passive income. By purchasing property and renting it out, you can create a steady stream of income each month. The key is to choose properties in desirable locations, manage them efficiently, and ensure they're well-maintained to attract long-term tenants.
- **Real Estate Crowdfunding:** If you're not ready to manage a property yourself, real estate crowdfunding platforms allow you to invest in real estate projects with other investors.

This way, you can earn passive income from real estate without the responsibilities of property management.

2. **Dividend Stocks and Investments:**
   - **Invest in Dividend-Paying Stocks:** Dividend stocks are shares in companies that pay out a portion of their profits to shareholders. By investing in a diversified portfolio of dividend-paying stocks, you can earn regular income from your investments while also benefiting from potential capital gains.
   - **Peer-to-Peer Lending:** Platforms like LendingClub or Prosper allow you to lend money to individuals or small businesses in exchange for interest payments. This can be a good way to generate passive income, though it's important to understand the risks involved.

3. **Create and Sell Digital Products:**
   - **E-books, Courses, and Templates:** If you have expertise in a particular area, consider creating digital products like e-books, online courses, or templates. Once created, these products can be sold repeatedly, generating passive income with each sale.
   - **Affiliate Marketing:** By promoting other people's products on your blog, social media, or website, you can earn commissions on sales made through your affiliate links. This is a popular passive income strategy for bloggers and online influencers.

Real-Life Example: Building Passive Income with Digital Products

Pat Flynn, the founder of Smart Passive Income, has successfully built a significant income stream by creating and selling digital products. Through his blog, podcast, and online courses, Flynn earns passive income by sharing his knowledge and expertise with a global audience. His success story illustrates how digital products can be a powerful source of passive income, allowing you to earn money while you sleep.

Final Thoughts: Passive Income is Key to Financial Freedom

Building passive income streams is a smart way to achieve financial freedom. By investing in assets that generate ongoing income, you can create financial security and reduce your dependence on active income. Whether it's through real estate, investments, or digital products, the key is to start building passive income today and watch it grow over time

Chapter 32:
Mindset Shifts for Financial Success

Success in life and finances starts in the mind. The way you think about money, opportunities, and your own potential can either propel you forward or hold you back. The most successful people understand that achieving financial success isn't just about strategy; it's about mindset. By shifting your mindset, you can break free from limiting beliefs, embrace opportunities, and create the financial future you desire.

The Power of a Wealth-Oriented Mindset

A wealth-oriented mindset is about believing that you have the power to create and control your financial destiny. It's about viewing money as a tool for freedom, not just a necessity, and understanding that abundance is possible for anyone willing to put in the effort.

Key Mindset Shifts for Financial Success

1. From Scarcity to Abundance:

- **Believe in Abundance:** Many people grow up with a scarcity mindset, believing that resources are limited and that wealth is only for the lucky few. Shifting to an abundance mindset means believing that there are enough opportunities, money, and success to go around. This shift allows you to see possibilities where others see limitations.
- **Practice Gratitude:** Gratitude is a powerful tool for cultivating an abundance mindset. By focusing on what you have rather than what you lack, you create a positive cycle that attracts more opportunities and success into your life.

2. **From Fixed to Growth:**
   - **Embrace the Growth Mindset:** A fixed mindset believes that your abilities and intelligence are static. In contrast, a growth mindset believes that you can develop your skills, intelligence, and financial acumen through effort and learning. This mindset encourages continuous improvement and resilience in the face of challenges.
   - **See Failures as Learning Opportunities:** Instead of fearing failure, view it as a necessary part of the learning process. Each setback is an opportunity to learn, adjust your approach, and come back stronger. This shift in perspective can significantly boost your financial success.

3. **From Immediate Gratification to Long-Term Vision:**
   - **Think Long-Term:** Financial success often requires delaying gratification in favor of long-term goals. This might mean saving instead of spending, investing in your future rather than indulging in short-term pleasures, or building a business that pays off over time. Cultivating a long-term vision helps you stay focused on your ultimate financial goals.
   - **Set Clear, Achievable Goals:** Having clear financial goals gives you direction and purpose. Break down your long-term goals into smaller, achievable steps, and celebrate each milestone along the way. This keeps you motivated and on track.

4. **From Passive to Proactive:**
   - **Take Control of Your Financial Future:** Don't wait for opportunities to come to you—go out and create them. A proactive mindset means taking responsibility for your financial success and actively seeking ways to improve your situation. This could involve learning new skills, networking, investing, or starting a side business.

- **Overcome Limiting Beliefs:** Many people are held back by limiting beliefs about money, such as "I'm not good with money" or "I'll never be wealthy." Identify these beliefs and replace them with empowering thoughts like "I can learn to manage money" or "Wealth is possible for me."

Real-Life Example: The Power of Mindset Shifts

Consider the story of Jim Carrey, who famously wrote himself a check for $10 million for "acting services rendered" when he was a struggling actor. He dated the check three years into the future, visualized his success daily, and continued working towards his goal. Three years later, Carrey received a $10 million paycheck for his role in Dumb and Dumber. His belief in his own potential and his commitment to his goal are powerful examples of how mindset shifts can lead to financial success.

Final Thoughts: Your Mindset is Your Wealth

Your financial success begins with your mindset. By shifting from scarcity to abundance, from a fixed to a growth mindset, and from immediate gratification to long-term vision, you can unlock your potential and create the financial future you desire. Remember, the most important changes you can make are in your thinking. When you change your mindset, you change your life.

Chapter 33:

Customers Are So Dumb (But That's Your Opportunity)

At first glance, it might seem harsh to say that "customers are so dumb." But this provocative statement highlights a crucial reality in sales: many customers lack the knowledge, expertise, or insight to make the best purchasing decisions on their own. This isn't a criticism—it's an opportunity. As a sales professional, your job is to educate, guide, and sometimes even protect your customers from making poor choices. By understanding their gaps in knowledge, you can position yourself as a trusted advisor and drive better sales outcomes.

Why Customers Often Make Poor Decisions

1. **Information Overload:**

- **Too Much Noise:** In today's digital age, customers are bombarded with information from every direction. This overwhelming amount of data can lead to confusion, misinterpretation, and poor decision-making. When faced with too many choices or conflicting information, customers may default to what's easiest rather than what's best.
- **Misinformation:** The internet is rife with misinformation, outdated advice, and biased reviews. Customers may come to you with preconceived notions that are completely off-base. It's your role to gently correct these misunderstandings and provide them with accurate, relevant information.

2. **Emotional Decision-Making:**
   - **Impulse Buying:** Many customers make decisions based on emotion rather than logic. They may buy something because it makes them feel good in the moment, without considering whether it's the right choice in the long run. Understanding this can help you steer the conversation toward more thoughtful, rational decisions.
   - **Fear and Anxiety:** Customers often fear making the wrong choice, leading to analysis paralysis or hasty decisions. By acknowledging their emotions and providing reassurance, you can help them make more confident and informed choices.

3. **Lack of Expertise:**
   - **Uninformed Choices:** Customers aren't experts in your field—that's why they come to you. They might not understand the nuances of the products or services you offer, leading them to make uninformed choices. Your role is to bridge that knowledge gap by explaining complex concepts in simple, relatable terms.
   - **Overconfidence:** Sometimes, customers believe they know more than they actually do, leading them to make decisions that aren't in their best interest. It's important to diplomatically challenge these assumptions and guide them toward better options.

How to Turn "Dumb" Customers into Smart Buyers

1. **Education Through Engagement:**
   - **Be the Expert:** Position yourself as a knowledgeable resource who can simplify complex information. Provide clear, concise explanations that make it easy for customers to understand the value of your products or services. Use

analogies, stories, and examples to make abstract concepts concrete.
- **Interactive Demos:** Use demonstrations, hands-on experiences, and visual aids to help customers grasp the benefits of your offerings. Interactive learning is often more effective than verbal explanations alone.

2. **Guided Decision-Making:**

- **Ask the Right Questions:** Help customers clarify their needs by asking insightful questions. This not only helps you understand their situation better but also encourages them to think more critically about their choices.
- **Present Simplified Options:** Too many choices can overwhelm customers. Offer a curated selection of options that best meet their needs, and explain the pros and cons of each. By simplifying their decision-making process, you help them make more confident choices.

3. **Build Trust Through Transparency:**

- **Honesty is Key:** Be transparent about what your product or service can and cannot do. Customers appreciate honesty, and this builds trust. Even if your offering isn't the perfect fit, they'll remember your integrity and be more likely to return in the future.
- **Address Misconceptions:** If a customer has incorrect information, correct it respectfully. Use evidence, case studies, or expert opinions to back up your claims. This not only educates the customer but also reinforces your credibility.

Real-World Example: Educating Customers for Success

Consider how Apple educates its customers. Many people don't fully understand the technical details of their devices, but Apple simplifies the technology through easy-to-understand language, intuitive design, and in-store workshops. By educating their customers, Apple turns potential confusion into brand loyalty.

Final Thoughts: Your Role as the Educator

It's easy to get frustrated when customers don't seem to "get it," but remember that their lack of knowledge is your opportunity. By educating, guiding, and simplifying the decision-making process, you can transform "dumb" customers into smart, loyal buyers. Your expertise is what they need—so embrace the role of educator, and watch your sales thrive.

Chapter 34:

Understanding Customer Behavior: The Key to Tailored Sales Strategies

Sales success hinges not just on what you sell, but on how well you understand the people you're selling to. In an era where customers are more informed and discerning than ever, understanding customer behavior is the cornerstone of creating tailored sales strategies that resonate. By deeply understanding what drives your customers' decisions, you can craft approaches that speak directly to their needs, desires, and pain points, making your offer irresistible.

Why Understanding Customer Behavior is Crucial

Every buying decision is influenced by a complex web of emotions, motivations, and external factors. When you understand these elements, you can predict what will drive your customers to say "yes." It's not just about knowing your customer on a surface level—age, gender, or occupation—but about digging deeper into their psychological makeup, their values, and their fears. This understanding allows you to position your product or service as the perfect solution to their unique problems.

Key Elements of Customer Behavior

1. **Psychological Triggers:**

   o **Emotional Drivers:** Emotions are powerful motivators in the decision-making process. Understanding what emotions your product or service evokes can help you tap into your customers' desires and fears. For instance, selling a luxury item isn't just about the product; it's about the status, security, or happiness it brings. By understanding these

emotional drivers, you can tailor your messaging to evoke the right feelings and increase the likelihood of a sale.
- **Cognitive Biases:** Customers are influenced by cognitive biases—mental shortcuts that affect their perceptions and decisions. Recognizing these biases, such as the tendency to favor familiar brands (familiarity bias) or the desire to avoid loss (loss aversion), can help you craft messages that align with how customers naturally think. For example, emphasizing what customers stand to lose by not choosing your product can be more compelling than highlighting what they will gain.

2. **Cultural and Social Influences:**
- **Cultural Values:** Cultural background heavily influences what customers value and how they make decisions. Understanding the cultural context of your target audience allows you to frame your product in a way that aligns with their beliefs and values. For example, a marketing strategy that emphasizes community and family might resonate more with a collectivist culture, while an approach focused on individuality and personal success might be more effective in individualist cultures.
- **Social Proof:** People often look to others to determine their own actions, especially in uncertain situations. Highlighting testimonials, case studies, or endorsements from influencers can provide the social proof needed to reassure potential customers and drive them toward a purchase. In a world where online reviews and recommendations play a significant role, leveraging social proof can be a powerful tool in your sales strategy.

3. **Behavioral Segmentation:**
- **Customer Segmentation by Behavior:** Instead of simply segmenting customers by demographics, consider their

behaviors—how they interact with your brand, their purchase history, and their engagement with your content. Behavioral segmentation allows for more precise targeting, ensuring your sales strategies are as effective as possible. For example, customers who frequently browse your website but haven't made a purchase might respond well to a limited-time discount, while loyal customers might appreciate a reward program.
- **Predictive Insights:** Use data and analytics to predict future customer behavior. By understanding patterns in past behavior, you can anticipate customer needs and tailor your sales approach to meet those needs before they even arise. Predictive modeling can help you identify which customers are most likely to convert and what strategies will be most effective in reaching them.

Strategies for Tailoring Sales Approaches Based on Customer Behavior

1. **Personalized Marketing:**

- **Customization is Key:** Today's customers expect personalized experiences. Use the insights you've gained from understanding customer behavior to create marketing messages that speak directly to individual customers. This could involve personalized emails, custom product recommendations, or targeted ads that address specific pain points. Personalization makes customers feel valued and increases their likelihood of making a purchase.
- **Empathy in Communication:** Empathy is a powerful tool in sales. When you show customers that you understand their struggles and genuinely care about solving their problems, they are more likely to trust you and your brand. Tailor your communication to be empathetic, addressing their concerns and offering solutions that feel personal and sincere. This

approach not only builds trust but also fosters long-term loyalty.

2. **Behavioral Triggers in Sales Funnels:**
   - **Incorporate Behavioral Triggers:** Use behavioral triggers within your sales funnels to guide customers toward a purchase. For example, scarcity (limited-time offers) can create urgency, while reminders based on browsing history can nudge customers back toward a purchase they were considering. Understanding the behavioral triggers that resonate with your audience allows you to create more effective sales funnels.
   - **A/B Testing for Optimization:** Continuously test different approaches to see what resonates best with your audience. A/B testing allows you to compare variations of your sales messages or landing pages to determine which version drives more conversions, helping you refine your strategies based on actual customer behavior. This data-driven approach ensures that your sales strategies are always optimized for maximum effectiveness.

3. **Continuous Feedback Loop:**
   - **Gather and Analyze Feedback:** Customer feedback is a goldmine of information about their behavior and preferences. Regularly seek out feedback through surveys, reviews, and direct conversations, and use this data to refine your sales approach. Understanding what your customers like and dislike about your current approach can help you make necessary adjustments and improve overall satisfaction.
   - **Adapt and Iterate:** The market is constantly changing, and so are customer behaviors. Stay agile by continuously adapting your strategies based on the feedback you receive. This iterative approach ensures that your sales tactics

evolve in line with customer expectations and market dynamics. By staying responsive and flexible, you can maintain a competitive edge and continue to meet your customers' needs.

Real-World Example: Amazon's Customer-Centric Approach

Amazon is a master at understanding and leveraging customer behavior. Through their sophisticated recommendation algorithms, Amazon analyzes customer behavior, such as past purchases and browsing history, to suggest products that customers are likely to buy. This personalized approach has been a significant factor in Amazon's ability to convert casual browsers into loyal customers. By continuously refining their algorithms and staying in tune with customer preferences, Amazon has created a seamless shopping experience that feels personalized to each individual user.

Final Thoughts: Align Your Sales Strategy with Customer Behavior

Understanding customer behavior is the foundation of tailored sales strategies that work. When you know what drives your customers, you can align your approach to meet their needs and desires, ultimately leading to more successful sales outcomes. By continuously learning about your customers and adapting your strategies accordingly, you'll not only boost your sales but also build lasting relationships that drive long-term success.

Chapter 35:
Value Your Worth: Get What You Deserve

Pricing your product or service is one of the most critical decisions you can make as a business owner. Price too low, and you risk undervaluing your offering and leaving money on the table. Price too high, and you might scare away potential customers. This chapter explores strategies to ensure you value your worth and get what you deserve.

Understanding the Psychology of Pricing

Pricing is not just about numbers—it's about perception. The price you set communicates value to your customers, and their willingness to pay is often influenced by how they perceive that value. If you undervalue your product or service, customers might question its quality. Conversely, a higher price can sometimes imply superior quality or exclusivity.

Key Strategies for Effective Pricing

1. **Know Your Costs and Margins:**

- **Cover All Costs:** Ensure your pricing covers all your costs, including materials, labor, overhead, and any other expenses. Additionally, factor in your desired profit margin to ensure the business remains profitable.
- **Understand Margins:** Calculate your gross margin and net margin to understand the profitability of each product or service. Gross margin is the difference between sales and the cost of goods sold, while net margin accounts for all expenses, including operating costs.

2. **Research the Market:**
   - **Competitor Analysis:** Look at what your competitors are charging for similar products or services. While you don't need to match their prices exactly, understanding the market range can help you position your pricing competitively.
   - **Understand Your Target Audience:** Different segments of the market have different price sensitivities. Luxury buyers, for example, are often willing to pay more for premium quality, while budget-conscious consumers might prioritize affordability.

3. **Highlight the Value:**
   - **Communicate Benefits:** Focus on the value your product or service provides. Highlight how it solves a problem, improves life, or offers benefits that justify the price. For example, if your product saves customers time, calculate that time saved into monetary value.
   - **Use Value-Based Pricing:** Set your prices based on the perceived value to the customer rather than just the cost of production. This approach allows you to charge more if your product or service delivers significant value.

4. **Create Tiered Pricing Options:**
   - **Offer Choices:** Provide different pricing tiers for different levels of service or product features. For example, a basic, premium, and deluxe package allows customers to choose the option that best fits their needs and budget. This strategy can also make the higher-priced options seem more attractive.
   - **Anchor Pricing:** Use a high-priced option as an anchor to make other prices seem more reasonable. For instance, if you offer a product at $100, $200, and $500, the $200 option might seem like the best value compared to the high anchor.

Handling Pricing Objections

Customers may sometimes question or push back on your pricing. How you handle these objections can make or break the sale.

1. **Justify the Price:**
   - **Break Down the Costs:** Show customers what goes into the pricing. For instance, explain the quality of materials, the craftsmanship, or the exceptional service that justifies the cost. Transparency builds trust and helps customers see the value they're getting.
   - **Highlight Long-Term Value:** Emphasize the long-term savings or benefits of choosing your product or service. For example, a higher initial investment might save the customer money over time due to durability, efficiency, or added features.

2. **Offer Payment Options:**
   - **Flexible Payments:** Provide installment plans, financing, or other flexible payment options that make it easier for customers to afford your product or service. This can reduce the price barrier and make higher-priced offerings more accessible.

Case Study: Apple's Premium Pricing Strategy

Apple is known for its premium pricing strategy, yet its products continue to be in high demand. Apple doesn't just sell electronics—they sell a brand, an experience, and an ecosystem. By focusing on design, innovation, and user experience, Apple justifies its higher prices and maintains a strong customer base willing to pay a premium for their products.

Final Thoughts: Know Your Worth, Charge What You Deserve

Pricing isn't just about numbers; it's about understanding the value you bring to the table and ensuring that value is reflected in your pricing. By setting prices that reflect the true worth of your products or services, you not only ensure profitability but also communicate to your customers that what you offer is worth every penny. Remember, it's not just about making a sale—it's about making a sale that supports the growth and sustainability of your business.

Chapter 36:

Give More Than You Charge: The Secret to Lasting Success

In the competitive world of sales and business, there's a principle that sets the most successful entrepreneurs apart from the rest: the commitment to giving more value than you charge. This concept might seem counterintuitive at first—after all, isn't the goal to maximize profits? However, the secret to long-term success lies in overdelivering on value. When you consistently provide more than what your customers expect, you build trust, loyalty, and a brand that people can't help but recommend to others.

The Power of Overdelivering

When you give more than what you charge, you're not just making a sale; you're building a relationship. Customers who feel they've received exceptional value are more likely to return, refer others, and become advocates for your brand. Here's why overdelivering is so powerful:

- **Trust and Loyalty:** By providing more value than expected, you establish a foundation of trust. Customers feel that you genuinely care about their needs, not just their money. This trust translates into loyalty, with customers returning to you repeatedly because they know they're getting the best deal.
- **Word-of-Mouth Marketing:** When customers are thrilled with the value they've received, they're likely to share their experience with others. This kind of organic marketing is priceless—it's more credible and effective than any advertisement you could pay for.
- **Brand Reputation:** Overdelivering helps you build a reputation as a business that goes above and beyond. This

reputation can set you apart from competitors and attract new customers who are seeking a reliable and trustworthy provider.

How to Overdeliver on Value

So how do you consistently give more than you charge? It's about more than just offering discounts or freebies—it's about understanding your customers' needs and exceeding their expectations in meaningful ways. Here's how:

1. **Understand Your Customers Deeply:**

- **Listen and Learn:** Take the time to really understand your customers' pain points, needs, and desires. Conduct surveys, engage with them on social media, or simply ask for feedback. The better you understand them, the more effectively you can tailor your offerings to exceed their expectations.
- **Personalize Your Service:** One size doesn't fit all. Personalization is key to making customers feel valued. Whether it's through personalized recommendations, follow-up emails, or tailored discounts, showing that you understand and cater to their individual needs makes a huge difference.

2. **Deliver Quality That Exceeds Expectations:**

- **Focus on Excellence:** Quality should never be compromised. Whether it's the products you sell or the services you offer, ensure that everything you provide is of the highest standard. Customers will notice the difference, and they'll appreciate that you're committed to delivering excellence.
- **Go the Extra Mile:** Sometimes, overdelivering means doing something unexpected. It could be as simple as adding a handwritten thank-you note to an order, offering a surprise

bonus service, or providing extra support after a purchase. These small gestures can make a big impact.

3. **Create a Memorable Experience:**
   - **Enhance the Customer Journey:** From the moment a customer interacts with your brand, ensure that every touchpoint is positive, easy, and memorable. Simplify the buying process, provide excellent customer service, and follow up after the sale to ensure satisfaction.
   - **Surprise and Delight:** Introduce elements of surprise into your customer interactions. This could be a free upgrade, a bonus product, or a loyalty reward. Surprises like these not only exceed expectations but also create a sense of delight that customers associate with your brand.

4. **Provide Ongoing Value:**
   - **Offer Continued Support:** Don't disappear after the sale. Offer ongoing support and resources that help your customers get the most out of their purchase. This could include how-to guides, webinars, or access to a customer community.
   - **Stay Engaged:** Keep the relationship alive by staying in touch with your customers. Regularly share valuable content, updates, and offers that are relevant to their needs. This ongoing engagement reinforces the value they receive from your brand.

Case Study: Zappos – The Gold Standard of Overdelivering

Zappos, the online shoe retailer, is often cited as a gold standard for customer service. They're famous for their commitment to overdelivering on value. Zappos offers free shipping and returns, but they also go beyond this by upgrading shipping to faster delivery at no extra charge, offering 24/7 customer service, and even allowing customers to return items up to a year after purchase. Their dedication to exceeding customer expectations has earned them a loyal customer base and a reputation as one of the most customer-centric companies in the world.

Final Thoughts: The Long-Term Benefits of Giving More

When you give more than you charge, you're investing in the long-term success of your business. It's not just about making a sale today—it's about building a brand that people trust, love, and return to time and again. Overdelivering on value might require more effort upfront, but the returns in customer loyalty, word-of-mouth marketing, and brand reputation are invaluable. So, commit to giving more, and watch as your business grows stronger and more successful with each satisfied customer.

Chapter 37:

Master the Art of Negotiation: Closing Deals with Confidence

In sales, negotiation is where the real game begins. It's the difference between closing a small deal and landing a life-changing one. The most successful salespeople understand that negotiation is not just about price—it's about value, psychology, and confidence. To become a master negotiator, you need to own the room, control the conversation, and close the deal with authority.

Why Confidence is Key in Negotiation

Before diving into tactics, understand one fundamental truth: Confidence sells. If you're not confident in your offer, neither will your prospect be. Negotiation is about controlling the narrative, and you can't control anything if you're hesitant or unsure. When you speak with conviction, it reassures the buyer that your product is worth every cent.

But confidence doesn't come naturally to everyone. The key is preparation. Know your product inside and out, understand your customer's pain points, and be ready to counter any objections. The more prepared you are, the more confident you'll be.

The Power of Silence: Talk Less, Listen More

A rookie mistake in negotiation is talking too much. The more you talk, the more leverage you give away. One of the most powerful tactics in negotiation is **silence**. When you make your offer or present your counter, shut up. Let the silence create pressure. In most cases, the other party will fill the silence by either agreeing or offering valuable information that you can use to your advantage.

Example: Imagine you're negotiating a price, and you say, "I can offer this product for $1,000." Then, stop talking. Let the silence sit. More often than not, the other person will speak first, and they might say something like, "That seems high, but maybe if we...," giving you valuable insight into where their mind is.

Control the Frame: Lead the Negotiation

The one who controls the frame controls the negotiation. By "frame," we mean how the discussion is shaped. When you lead the conversation, you keep the buyer focused on value, not price. Every time they try to haggle or bring the conversation back to cost, reframe the discussion around the **value** your product provides.

Example: If the buyer says, "Can we reduce the price by 10%?" you could respond with, "I understand the concern about pricing, but let's focus on what you're getting here. This product will save you 20 hours a week, and within six months, you'll see a return on investment. The question isn't about price—it's about the value of your time and growth."

Anchoring: Set the Price High

One of the most proven negotiation techniques is **anchoring**. Anchoring means starting with a higher-than-expected offer so that any counter-offer feels like a deal to the buyer. When you set the bar high, you leave room for negotiation, but more importantly, you set the expectation that your product or service is of top value.

Example: Let's say you're selling a service and expect the deal to close at $2,000. You start by proposing $2,500. The client might try to negotiate down, but even if they push, they're negotiating from a higher starting point, and $2,000 will suddenly seem like a deal to them.

Give to Get: Concessions with Purpose

Negotiation isn't about winning at all costs. It's about creating a win-win scenario that leaves both parties satisfied. One of the best ways to create this is by giving concessions—but only if you get something in return. Don't give away value for free. If the buyer asks for a discount or extra service, attach a condition.

Example: If a client says, "Can you give us a 10% discount?" reply with, "I can do that, but in return, I'd like to lock in a longer-term contract." This way, you maintain value while giving the client something they want.

Proven Examples of Negotiation Success

1. **Steve Jobs and Apple:** Steve Jobs was a master of negotiation. When developing the original iPhone, Jobs wanted the best glass for the screen. He approached Corning, the company known for Gorilla Glass, which was still in development. Jobs wasn't just buying a product—he was negotiating an investment in the future of Apple's ecosystem. He told Corning's CEO, "We don't have time, we need it in six months." Corning had never produced such a large volume of glass before, but Jobs' unwavering confidence and vision convinced them to fast-track the project. The result? Apple revolutionized the smartphone industry.
2. **Elon Musk and Tesla:** When Elon Musk was trying to keep Tesla afloat in its early years, he approached investors with extreme confidence, even when the company was on the brink of collapse. His negotiations with venture capitalists

and suppliers weren't about immediate returns—they were about the long-term vision of revolutionizing the automotive industry. Musk's ability to negotiate from a position of vision and confidence led to continued investments that helped Tesla become the giant it is today.

Take Control of the Terms

One trick expert negotiators use is controlling the terms, not just the price. By adding or removing elements from the deal, you can keep the price fixed while still providing value. For example, if a buyer asks for a discount, offer to keep the price the same but throw in a free month of service or an extra feature. This way, you maintain the integrity of the deal and show flexibility without lowering your price.

Example: If a customer says, "I can't pay more than $500," you could say, "I understand that budget is a concern. What if we kept the price at $500 but offered you a premium package for the first three months?"

Final Thoughts: Negotiation is an Art, Not a Battle

Negotiation isn't about outsmarting or defeating the other side—it's about finding common ground and closing the deal in a way that leaves everyone satisfied. The key is to approach every negotiation with preparation, confidence, and a value-focused mindset. Remember, the best negotiators are the ones who control the conversation, listen more than they talk, and know when to push and when to concede.

Master the art of negotiation, and you'll not only close more deals—you'll close them with confidence, knowing you've secured the best possible outcome for both you and your client.

Chapter 38:

The 80/20 Rule: How It Works in Sales and Business

The 80/20 rule, also known as the Pareto Principle, is a powerful concept that can transform the way you approach sales and business. At its core, the 80/20 rule suggests that 80% of your results come from just 20% of your efforts. This principle is not just a theory—it's a proven strategy that successful businesses and sales professionals use to maximize efficiency, focus on what truly matters, and drive significant results. In this chapter, we'll explore how the 80/20 rule applies to sales and business, and how you can leverage it to achieve greater success.

Understanding the 80/20 Rule

1. **The Pareto Principle Explained:**

- **Origins of the 80/20 Rule:** The 80/20 rule is named after Italian economist Vilfredo Pareto, who observed that 80% of Italy's wealth was owned by 20% of the population. This observation led to the realization that this ratio could be applied to many areas of life, particularly in business and sales.
- **The Power of Focus:** The essence of the 80/20 rule is that not all efforts are equal. A small percentage of your actions or inputs often lead to the majority of your outcomes or outputs. Recognizing this allows you to focus on the high-impact activities that drive the most significant results.

2. **Identifying the Vital Few:**

- **The 20% That Matters:** In sales, this might mean that 20% of your clients generate 80% of your revenue, or that 20%

of your products account for 80% of your profits. In business, it could mean that 20% of your efforts lead to 80% of your growth. The key is to identify which 20% of your activities are producing the majority of your success.
- **Eliminating the Trivial Many:** Once you've identified the 20% that matters, it's crucial to minimize or eliminate the 80% of activities that contribute little to your success. This doesn't mean ignoring important tasks, but rather streamlining your efforts to focus on what truly drives results.

Applying the 80/20 Rule to Sales

1. **Focus on High-Value Clients:**

- **Identify Your Top Customers:** Analyze your customer base to identify the 20% of clients who generate the most revenue. These high-value customers are your priority. Invest more time in nurturing these relationships, offering personalized service, and upselling relevant products or services.
- **Tailor Your Sales Strategy:** Develop sales strategies that specifically target these top customers. By focusing on their needs and providing exceptional value, you can increase their loyalty, drive repeat business, and maximize your sales potential.

2. **Optimize Your Sales Process:**

- **Streamline Your Efforts:** Look at your sales process and identify the 20% of activities that lead to the majority of your sales. This could be a specific lead generation tactic, a particular sales pitch, or a follow-up strategy that consistently converts. Focus on refining and optimizing these key activities to enhance your overall sales performance.

- **Delegate or Automate the Rest:** For the remaining 80% of tasks that don't contribute as much to your sales, consider delegating them to others or automating them where possible. This allows you to free up time and resources to concentrate on the activities that make the most significant impact.

Applying the 80/20 Rule to Business

1. **Product and Service Focus:**

- **Identify Your Best Sellers:** In many businesses, a small percentage of products or services generate the majority of profits. Identify these high-performing offerings and focus your marketing, sales, and development efforts on them. Consider scaling back or discontinuing lower-performing products to concentrate on what's truly driving your business forward.
- **Enhance the Customer Experience:** Focus on the 20% of customer interactions that lead to 80% of your customer satisfaction. This could involve refining your customer service protocols, improving your website's user experience, or streamlining your purchase process. By enhancing these critical touchpoints, you can significantly boost customer loyalty and retention.

2. **Time and Resource Management:**

- **Prioritize High-Impact Tasks:** As a business leader, your time is valuable. Apply the 80/20 rule to your daily activities by prioritizing the tasks that have the most significant impact on your business's success. Whether it's strategic planning, networking, or product development, focus on the tasks that drive the most value.
- **Cut the Fat:** Eliminate or reduce the tasks and projects that consume time and resources but don't contribute much to your overall goals. This might mean outsourcing

administrative work, cutting down on unnecessary meetings, or streamlining your operations to focus on what matters most.

Real-World Example: Apple's Product Line

Apple is a prime example of a company that applies the 80/20 rule effectively. Despite being one of the world's largest tech companies, Apple focuses on a relatively small product line—iPhone, iPad, Mac, and a few other key products. These products generate the majority of Apple's revenue, allowing the company to focus its marketing, innovation, and sales efforts on these core items, rather than spreading itself thin across a vast range of offerings. This focus on the vital few has made Apple one of the most successful companies in the world.

Final Thoughts: Leverage the 80/20 Rule for Success

The 80/20 rule is more than just a principle—it's a strategy for maximizing your efficiency, focus, and results. By identifying the 20% of activities, clients, or products that drive the majority of your success, you can concentrate your efforts where they matter most. Whether in sales or business, applying the 80/20 rule will help you work smarter, not harder, and achieve greater success with less effort. Remember, it's not about doing more—it's about doing what matters most.

Chapter 39:

Give It Free, Charge Later

The strategy of giving something away for free may seem counterintuitive in a world driven by profit, but it's a tactic that has proven to be incredibly powerful in building customer bases and driving long-term revenue. "Free" is not just a price tag—it's a powerful hook that can create loyal customers, generate buzz, and set the stage for significant profits down the line. In this chapter, we'll explore how to strategically use the "give it free, charge later" approach to your advantage, with a special focus on the Jio SIM case study.

Why Giving It Free Works: The Long-Term Strategy

1. **Building a Customer Base:**

- **Instant Adoption:** Offering something valuable for free dramatically lowers the barrier to entry, encouraging people to try your product without hesitation. This approach allows you to quickly build a customer base, which is essential for creating market momentum.
- **Creating Habitual Use:** Once customers begin using your product, it becomes a part of their routine. By the time they're asked to pay, they've already integrated your product into their lives, making them more likely to continue using it even when a cost is involved.

2. **Creating a Buzz:**

- **Word of Mouth:** Free offers generate excitement and buzz, encouraging customers to spread the word. This organic promotion can exponentially increase your reach without the need for expensive marketing campaigns.
- **Perceived Value:** The idea of getting something for free often increases the perceived value of that item. Customers

feel they are receiving something valuable without any upfront cost, which makes them more appreciative and loyal when it comes time to pay.

The Jio SIM Case Study: A Masterclass in Free to Paid Strategy

In 2016, Reliance Jio revolutionized the Indian telecom industry by offering free 4G SIM cards with unlimited data, voice calls, and SMS for several months. This move was unprecedented and disrupted the entire market. Here's how Jio's "give it free, charge later" strategy played out:

1. **Rapid Market Penetration:**

- **Free for All:** Jio's free offer was irresistible. Millions of Indians flocked to get their hands on a Jio SIM, resulting in an unprecedented rate of adoption. Within months, Jio had acquired millions of users, making it the fastest-growing telecom company in the world at the time.
- **Building Infrastructure:** While Jio offered services for free, it simultaneously built a robust infrastructure to handle the growing user base. By the time the free period ended, Jio had established itself as a reliable service provider.

2. **Monetization Post Free Period:**

- **Transition to Paid Plans:** Once Jio had a massive, loyal user base, it introduced paid plans that were competitively priced. By then, users had already integrated Jio into their daily lives, making the transition to paid services seamless. The initial free offer created a strong foundation for long-term revenue.
- **Continued Value Proposition:** Even after the free period ended, Jio continued to offer more value than its competitors, ensuring that customers felt they were getting

more for their money. This strategy helped Jio retain its massive customer base and continue growing its market share.

How to Implement the "Give It Free, Charge Later" Strategy

1. **Identify What to Offer for Free:**

- **Choose High-Value Offerings:** The key is to offer something that genuinely adds value to the customer's life. Whether it's a free trial of a premium service, a valuable product sample, or an educational resource, the free offering should showcase the best of what you have to offer.
- **Set Clear Limits:** It's important to define what's free and what's not. Whether it's a limited-time offer, a basic version of a product, or a specific feature set, make sure customers understand the boundaries of the free offer and what they'll need to pay for in the future.

2. **Plan for the Transition to Paid:**

- **Communicate Early:** Don't spring the paid offer on customers out of nowhere. Start communicating the value of the paid service early in the customer journey. Explain the benefits of upgrading and why it's worth the investment.
- **Offer Incentives:** To ease the transition from free to paid, offer special discounts, exclusive features, or bundled deals. These incentives can make the decision to pay feel like a natural and valuable next step.

3. **Focus on Long-Term Customer Relationships:**

- **Build Trust:** By offering something valuable for free, you build trust with your customers. This trust makes them more likely to stick with your product when it comes time to pay.

- **Continuous Engagement:** Keep engaging with your customers even after they've transitioned to the paid service. Offer ongoing value, whether through updates, new features, or excellent customer service, to ensure long-term loyalty.

Final Thoughts: Free as a Pathway to Profit

The "give it free, charge later" strategy isn't about losing money—it's about investing in your customer base and setting the stage for long-term profitability. By offering something of value for free, you lower the barriers to entry, build trust, and create a foundation for future sales. The Jio SIM case study is a testament to how powerful this approach can be when executed correctly. So, don't be afraid to give it free, because when done right, it leads to significant returns.

Chapter 40:

Do It Now or Regret Later

Procrastination is the silent killer of success. In sales, hesitation can mean the difference between closing a deal and watching it slip through your fingers. The window of opportunity is often small, and those who seize the moment are the ones who come out on top. This chapter is about cultivating a sense of urgency—not just for your customers, but for yourself. The mantra is simple: **"Do it now, or regret it later."**

The High Cost of Hesitation

1. **Opportunities Don't Wait:**

- **The Value of Speed:** In sales, timing is everything. Opportunities can vanish as quickly as they appear. Whether it's following up on a lead, closing a deal, or launching a new campaign, speed is crucial. The longer you wait, the more likely it is that your competition will swoop in and steal the deal.
- **Lost Momentum:** Hesitation kills momentum. When you delay taking action, you lose the energy and enthusiasm that can drive a sale forward. Customers can sense hesitation, and it can make them second-guess their decision to buy. Momentum is your friend—once you have it, don't lose it.

2. **The Pain of Regret:**

- **Missed Opportunities:** One of the most painful feelings in business is looking back at an opportunity you had and realizing you let it slip away. Regret is often more intense than the fear that causes hesitation in the first place. By acting now, you eliminate the chance for regret later.

- **What Ifs:** Every opportunity missed is a "what if" that could haunt you. What if you had made that call? What if you had taken that meeting?

3. **The Pain of Regret:**

- **Missed Opportunities:** One of the most painful feelings in business is looking back at an opportunity you had and realizing you let it slip away. Regret is often more intense than the fear that causes hesitation in the first place. By acting now, you eliminate the chance for regret later.
- **What Ifs:** Every opportunity missed is a "what if" that could haunt you. What if you had made that call? What if you had taken that meeting? What if you had launched that campaign sooner? These questions can linger, impacting your confidence and decision-making in the future.

The Power of Immediate Action

1. **Seize the Moment:**

- **Create a Bias for Action:** Successful salespeople develop a bias for action. They don't wait for the perfect moment; they create it. When a potential client shows interest, they move quickly to close the deal. When a challenge arises, they address it head-on. By acting swiftly, you not only increase your chances of success but also demonstrate confidence and decisiveness.
- **Capitalize on Enthusiasm:** When a customer shows interest, that's the moment to strike. Their enthusiasm is at its peak, and they're most likely to say "yes." Waiting too long can cause that enthusiasm to fade, leading to lost sales. The key is to act while the customer is excited and engaged.

2. **Build Urgency Into Your Sales Process:**

- **Create Urgency for the Customer:** One of the most effective sales tactics is to create a sense of urgency for the customer.

Limited-time offers, countdowns, and scarcity tactics can motivate customers to act now rather than later. When customers feel that they might miss out, they're more likely to make a quick decision.
- **Don't Overthink It:** Overthinking leads to hesitation, which can kill sales. Trust your instincts, make decisions quickly, and move forward with confidence. Perfection is the enemy of progress, and in sales, progress is everything.

Real-World Example: Nike's "Just Do It" Philosophy

Nike's famous slogan, "Just Do It," isn't just a marketing tagline—it's a philosophy that drives action. Nike encourages athletes and customers alike to push past hesitation and take action now, whether it's hitting the gym, starting a new sport, or making a purchase. This sense of urgency and action has been key to Nike's brand identity and success. They don't wait—they do.

Final Thoughts: No More Waiting—Act Now

The difference between those who succeed and those who don't often comes down to one thing: action. Those who act now, who take risks, and who seize opportunities are the ones who achieve their goals. In sales, waiting is the enemy. By embracing a mindset of immediate action, you not only increase your chances of success but also eliminate the possibility of future regret. Remember, it's better to act now and fail than to do nothing and wonder what could have been. So, do it now, or regret it later.

Chapter 41:

Content is King: Make Your Mark in the Digital World

In the vast and ever-evolving digital landscape, content reigns supreme. It's the driving force behind influence, authority, and income. If you want to make a lasting impact online, your content needs to be more than just good—it needs to be unforgettable. This isn't about blending in; it's about standing out and making your mark in a world where everyone is vying for attention.

Why Content Defines Your Digital Presence

Let's be direct: without standout content, you're just another voice lost in the noise. Your content is what differentiates you from the competition. It's your platform to communicate, persuade, and connect with your audience on a deeper level. When done right, content is the catalyst that transforms you from a participant in the digital world to a leader within it.

The Essential Elements of Impactful Content

1. **Be Unapologetically Authentic:**

- **No Holding Back:** Authenticity cuts through the clutter. People gravitate towards content that feels real and genuine. Share your true experiences, the lessons you've learned, and the perspectives that are uniquely yours. Authenticity builds trust and forges strong connections.
- **Own Your Narrative:** Your story is what sets you apart. Embrace it fully—whether it's your successes, your failures, or your unique journey. Your narrative is the foundation of your content, and when it resonates, it leaves a lasting impression.

2. **Craft Content That Resonates:**

   - **Quality Over Quantity:** Impact is more important than volume. A single piece of well-crafted content can resonate more deeply than a dozen mediocre efforts. Focus on creating content that is thoughtful, polished, and meaningful.
   - **Challenge the Norms:** Don't be afraid to push boundaries and offer perspectives that challenge the status quo. Memorable content often disrupts, provokes thought, and inspires change. Make your audience pause and consider a new viewpoint.

3. **Content with Purpose:**

   - **Clear Objectives:** Every piece of content should serve a purpose. Whether you're aiming to educate, inspire, or drive action, your content must be intentional and aligned with your broader goals. Purpose-driven content is compelling and powerful.
   - **Lead by Example:** Your content should guide your audience toward a desired outcome. Whether it's clicking a link, sharing a post, or making a purchase, make it clear what you want your audience to do next. A strong call to action is essential.

4. **Stay Ahead, Stay Relevant:**

   - **Innovate and Adapt:** The digital world moves quickly, and staying relevant requires constant innovation. Experiment with new content formats, explore emerging platforms, and always be ready to adapt to changing trends. Innovation keeps your content fresh and engaging.
   - **Data-Driven Decisions:** Use analytics to gain insights into what's working and what isn't. By understanding your audience's preferences, you can refine your content strategy to maximize impact. Data-driven content is both effective and efficient.

Real-World Example: Content That Creates a Legacy

Consider how Gary Vaynerchuk, or Gary Vee, has established his legacy through relentless content creation. He doesn't just post—he dominates platforms like YouTube, Instagram, and Twitter with content that is raw, insightful, and, most importantly, authentic. By staying true to himself and constantly innovating, Gary Vee has made a lasting mark on the digital world.

Final Thoughts: Leave Your Mark with Content

Content is the cornerstone of your digital presence. It's what will set you apart, drive your success, and make your mark in a crowded online world. So, don't just contribute—lead. Create content that commands attention, drives action, and solidifies your place as a true authority in your field. In the digital world, only those who dare to be bold and authentic truly make their mark.

Chapter 42:
Don't Consume, Just Sell

In the world of sales, there's a fundamental difference between those who succeed and those who struggle: the successful ones prioritize selling over consuming. It's easy to get caught up in consuming—whether it's content, advice, or even your competitors' strategies—but the real winners are the ones who focus on taking action and making sales happen. This chapter is about shifting your mindset from consumption to creation, from learning to doing, and from watching to selling.

The Pitfall of Overconsumption

We live in an age of information overload. There's always a new book to read, a new podcast to listen to, or a new webinar to attend. While learning is important, it's easy to fall into the trap of consuming too much and doing too little. The more you consume, the less time you have to apply what you've learned. In sales, action is everything—if you're not actively selling, you're falling behind.

1. **The Learning Trap:**
- **Endless Preparation:** Many salespeople believe they need to learn just one more thing before they're ready to start selling. This leads to endless preparation and a constant search for the next big idea, while real opportunities slip through their fingers.
- **Information Paralysis:** Consuming too much information can lead to analysis paralysis—when you have so many ideas, strategies, and tips swirling in your head that you can't decide where to start. This often results in inaction and missed sales.

2. **The Comparison Game:**
    - **Watching Competitors:** It's natural to keep an eye on your competition, but spending too much time analyzing their moves can distract you from making your own. If you're always focused on what others are doing, you're not focusing on what you can do better.
    - **Measuring Success by Others:** The more you consume content about other people's successes, the more likely you are to feel inadequate or overwhelmed. This can sap your motivation and prevent you from taking the bold actions necessary to succeed.

The Power of Action: Sell, Don't Wait

To succeed in sales, you need to shift your focus from consuming to doing. The best salespeople aren't the ones who know the most—they're the ones who act the most. They're out there making calls, sending emails, meeting clients, and closing deals while others are still researching and planning.

1. **Action Over Perfection:**
    - **Start Selling Now:** Stop waiting for the perfect moment, the perfect pitch, or the perfect product. Start selling with what you have right now. The act of selling itself will teach you more than any book or webinar ever could.
    - **Learn by Doing:** The best way to learn is by doing. Every sales interaction is an opportunity to improve, to refine your pitch, and to better understand your customers. Don't be afraid to make mistakes—each one is a stepping stone to success.

2. **Prioritize Selling Activities:**
    - **Focus on Revenue-Generating Tasks:** Your time should be spent on activities that directly contribute to making sales.

Whether it's prospecting, following up with leads, or closing deals, these tasks should take priority over consuming more information.
- **Set Actionable Goals:** Instead of setting goals around learning (like reading a certain number of books), set goals around selling (like making a certain number of calls or closing a certain number of deals). This will keep you focused on action and results.

3. **Measure Success by Your Own Progress:**

- **Track Your Sales Metrics:** Measure your success by your own performance, not by what others are doing. Track metrics like the number of sales calls made, meetings set, or deals closed. These are the numbers that matter—not how much content you've consumed.
- **Celebrate Your Wins:** Take the time to celebrate your successes, no matter how small. Each sale, each new client, and each milestone achieved is a step toward your larger goals. Recognizing your progress will keep you motivated and focused on what really matters.

Real-World Example: The Success of Doers

Consider entrepreneurs like Elon Musk or Richard Branson. They didn't build their empires by consuming endless content—they did it by taking massive action. They're constantly selling their vision, their products, and their companies. They don't wait for perfect conditions—they create them by doing, by selling, and by pushing forward no matter what.

Final Thoughts: Sell More, Consume Less

If you want to succeed in sales, you need to prioritize selling over consuming. Learning is important, but action is what drives results. The more time you spend selling, the closer you get to achieving your goals. So, stop waiting, stop watching, and start selling. The world doesn't need more consumers—it needs more doers. Be one of them.

Chapter 43:

Kill Procrastination — Or It Will Kill You

Procrastination is the silent assassin of dreams and goals. It creeps in, telling you that tomorrow is just as good as today, that there's plenty of time to get things done, that waiting for the perfect moment is wise. But here's the harsh truth: procrastination is not just a bad habit—it's a killer. In sales, in business, and in life, procrastination can be the difference between success and failure, between a deal closed and a deal lost. This chapter is about recognizing procrastination for what it is—a deadly threat—and taking immediate action to eliminate it from your life.

The Dangers of Procrastination

1. **Missed Opportunities:**

- **The Window Closes Fast:** Opportunities in sales are often fleeting. A lead that's hot today might cool off tomorrow. A client ready to buy now might find another solution if you wait too long. Procrastination closes the door on opportunities that could have been game-changers.
- **Lost Momentum:** Every time you put off a task, you lose momentum. Momentum is crucial in sales—it keeps you moving forward, driving toward your goals. When you procrastinate, you not only slow down, but you risk stopping altogether.

2. **The Accumulation of Stress:**

- **The Burden of Delays:** The more you procrastinate, the more tasks pile up. What could have been handled easily with timely action now becomes a mountain of stress. This

stress doesn't just impact your work—it affects your health, your mindset, and your overall well-being.
- **Paralysis by Analysis:** Procrastination often stems from overthinking. The more you think about a task, the more daunting it seems, leading to further delays. This vicious cycle can trap you in a state of inaction, where fear and anxiety keep you from making progress.

How to Kill Procrastination Before It Kills You

1. **Adopt an Action-Oriented Mindset:**

- **Start Now, Perfect Later:** The key to overcoming procrastination is to start, even if it's imperfect. Perfectionism is often the root of procrastination, but the truth is, action leads to improvement. Begin the task, learn as you go, and refine your approach along the way.
- **Break Tasks into Small Steps:** Large tasks can be overwhelming, which leads to procrastination. Break down your tasks into manageable steps. Each small victory builds momentum and makes the larger goal seem more achievable.

2. **Set Clear, Non-Negotiable Deadlines:**

- **Deadlines Create Pressure:** A task without a deadline is a task that will likely be put off. Set firm, non-negotiable deadlines for yourself and stick to them. The pressure of a deadline forces you to act, reducing the likelihood of procrastination.
- **Public Accountability:** Tell someone else about your deadline. When others are aware of your commitments, the pressure to deliver on time increases. This external accountability can be a powerful motivator to overcome procrastination.

3. **Prioritize and Focus:**
   - **Tackle High-Impact Tasks First:** Not all tasks are created equal. Focus on the tasks that have the most significant impact on your goals. Prioritizing these tasks ensures that even if you get sidetracked, you're making progress on what matters most.
   - **Eliminate Distractions:** Distractions fuel procrastination. Identify what pulls your attention away from your work—whether it's social media, email, or even unnecessary meetings—and eliminate or minimize these distractions during your work time.

Real-World Example: Steve Jobs' Relentless Focus

Steve Jobs was known for his ability to focus intensely on the task at hand. He didn't procrastinate or allow distractions to pull him away from his goals. His relentless focus and action-oriented mindset were key to building Apple into one of the most successful companies in the world. Jobs understood that procrastination was the enemy of innovation and success, and he took immediate action to kill it whenever it appeared.

Final Thoughts: Procrastination Is the Enemy

If you want to succeed, you need to treat procrastination as the enemy it is. Every moment you delay is a moment lost, an opportunity missed, a potential failure creeping closer. By adopting an action-oriented mindset, setting clear deadlines, and prioritizing your tasks, you can kill procrastination before it kills your dreams. Remember, in the battle for success, those who act win—those who wait, lose. So, kill procrastination now, before it kills you.

Chapter 44:
Don't Allow Money to Ruin Your Relations

Money is a powerful force. It has the potential to create incredible opportunities, but it can also be a destructive force if not managed wisely—especially when it comes to relationships. Mixing money with relationships is like playing with fire. It doesn't matter if it's family, friends, or business partners—bringing money into the equation can turn a strong bond into a ticking time bomb. This chapter explores why keeping money out of your relationships isn't just smart—it's essential. And to drive the point home, we'll dive into a real-life story that shows just how quickly things can go south when money gets involved.

The Dark Side of Mixing Money with Relationships

At its core, money is a tool, but when emotions, expectations, and power dynamics come into play, it can quickly become a weapon. Here's how money can ruin relationships and why it's best to keep finances separate:

- **Power Imbalance:**
  - **Turning Trust into Tension:** Lending money to someone close is like throwing a grenade into your relationship. What starts as an act of kindness can quickly turn into a source of tension. The borrower feels the weight of debt, and the lender starts to wonder when—or if—they'll get their money back. Trust is replaced by doubt, and the relationship starts to crack.
  - **Creating a Power Imbalance:** Lending money can create a power dynamic that's hard to shake. The borrower may feel beholden to the lender, leading to a shift in the relationship

dynamics. Suddenly, it's not about mutual respect—it's about one person having the upper hand.

- **Expectations and Assumptions:**
  - **Unspoken Expectations:** Money doesn't just come with strings attached—it comes with ropes. When you lend money, you're not just giving cash; you're creating expectations. You expect to be repaid, and maybe even appreciated. But when those expectations aren't met, resentment sets in, and that's when the relationship really starts to unravel.
  - **The Guilt Trip:** On the flip side, the lender might start to feel like they're being taken for a ride. Guilt and resentment can build up, poisoning the relationship from within. What started as a favor turns into a festering wound that's hard to heal.
- **Stress and Pressure:**
  - **Financial Strain Leading to Breakdown:** Financial stress is one of the leading causes of relationship breakdowns. When money is tight or financial goals are not aligned, it can lead to constant arguments, anxiety, and a breakdown in communication.

A Story of Friendship and Financial Fallout

Let's talk about Jake and Tom. Best friends since college, they did everything together. So when Tom hit a rough patch and asked Jake for a loan to help cover his mortgage, Jake didn't hesitate. After all, what are friends for? But months passed, and Tom hadn't paid back a cent. Jake didn't want to nag, but the silence was killing him. Meanwhile, Tom was drowning in guilt every time they hung out, so he started avoiding Jake altogether.

Eventually, the friendship fell apart—not because of a big fight, but because of the unspoken tension that money had created. What should have been a simple act of friendship turned into the death knell of their relationship. Jake lost a friend, and Tom lost the one person he thought he could count on. All because they let money get in the way.

The Bold Path: Protecting Your Relationships from Money's Influence

To prevent money from ruining your relationships, you need to take bold, proactive steps. Here's how you can protect your connections while still pursuing your financial goals:

1. **Draw the Line—No Exceptions:**
   - **Keep Finances Out:** Make it a rule—don't lend money to friends or family. It doesn't matter how close you are or how desperate they seem. The moment you cross that line, you're opening the door to potential disaster. Offer help in other ways—advice, time, emotional support—but keep your wallet out of it.
   - **Learn to Say No:** Saying no isn't easy, but it's necessary. It's better to set boundaries upfront than to risk ruining a relationship later. If someone you care about asks for money, explain your stance clearly and offer non-monetary support instead.

2. **Open and Honest Communication:**
   - **Lay Everything on the Table:** If you absolutely must involve money, transparency is key. Discuss your financial situation openly—your income, debts, spending habits, and financial goals. This sets the foundation for trust and ensures that everyone is on the same page.
   - **Set Clear Boundaries:** Establish what's off-limits when it comes to money. For example, if you're lending money to a

friend, be clear about the terms. If you're in a relationship, decide together how finances will be managed and who will be responsible for what.

3. **Value the Relationship Over the Money:**
   - **Put People First:** At the end of the day, relationships are more important than money. If a financial arrangement is starting to strain your relationship, be willing to walk away from the money to preserve the connection. Money comes and goes, but real relationships are priceless.
   - **Find Other Ways to Help:** Sometimes, the best way to help someone isn't with cash. Offer your time, your skills, or your advice instead. These forms of support can be just as valuable—if not more so—without the risk of damaging your relationship.

4. **Seek Professional Guidance:**
   - **Get an Outside Perspective:** Sometimes, a third-party perspective can help. Whether it's a financial advisor, mediator, or therapist, getting professional guidance can help you navigate tricky financial situations without damaging your relationship.
   - **Educate Yourself Together:** If you're in a relationship where financial literacy is an issue, take steps to learn together. Attend workshops, read books, or take courses that help you both understand and manage your finances better.

5. **Focus on Long-Term Harmony:**
   - **Align Financial Goals:** Whether in a personal relationship or business, aligning your financial goals is crucial. Discuss your long-term aspirations and how you can work together to achieve them. This creates a sense of partnership and shared purpose.

- **Celebrate Milestones:** Don't just focus on the challenges—celebrate the financial milestones you achieve together. Whether it's paying off debt, hitting a savings target, or securing a big client, these moments strengthen your bond and remind you why the relationship is worth protecting.

Final Thoughts: Don't Let Money Destroy What Matters

Jake and Tom's story is a cautionary tale. It's a reminder that money, for all its power, is not worth the price of a relationship. By keeping finances separate from your personal connections, you protect the bonds that truly matter. Remember, once money gets involved, it's not just about the dollars and cents—it's about trust, respect, and the future of your relationship. So, draw the line, keep your money where it belongs, and don't let something as replaceable as cash destroy something as irreplaceable as a strong relationship.

My Journey in Sales and Why I Wrote This Book

Sales has always been more than just a job for me—it's been a journey of learning, adapting, and growing. When I first started, like many of you, I didn't know the intricacies of closing deals or handling objections. I was just trying to figure out how to get my foot in the door. But over time, I realized that mastering sales isn't about having all the right answers from the start—it's about developing the right strategies, mindset, and most importantly, the confidence to keep pushing forward.

Through years of trial and error, I learned what works and what doesn't. I've seen firsthand how the power of storytelling, mastering negotiation, and understanding the psychology behind customer behavior can transform the way you sell. Those experiences, successes, and even failures became the foundation of *Sales God: Rise to the Top and Rule the Sales World.*

This book isn't just for people who've already made it in sales—it's for anyone, at any stage, who wants to understand how sales can change their life. Whether you're a beginner or an experienced professional, I've packed this book with actionable advice that you can implement right away. I wanted to make sure that this book didn't just talk about the theory of sales but gave you practical tools you can use to transform your business, your income, and your future.

Practical Steps to Implement What You've Learned

1. **Master Negotiation**: Start practicing the negotiation tips from this book in every interaction, whether in sales or personal life. The art of negotiation doesn't just happen in the boardroom—it's a skill that grows with daily practice.
2. **Build Relationships**: Reach out to your clients, past and present, and work on creating lasting relationships. Ask yourself: How can I add more value to them? What can I do to turn them into loyal advocates for my brand?
3. **Leverage Referrals**: Don't wait to ask for referrals—implement the strategies in the book right away. Word-of-mouth marketing can become your most powerful tool.
4. **Stay Adaptable**: In sales, you need to adapt to changes in the market, technology, and customer behavior. This book provides timeless principles, but don't forget to evolve with the times. Always look for new ways to improve your process.

My Journey and What You Can Learn from It

When I began writing this book, I reflected on my personal journey in sales. I didn't start as a sales expert; I was learning from scratch, making mistakes, and figuring it out along the way. But one thing remained constant: I never stopped pushing myself to learn and improve. I wasn't afraid to experiment, fail, and adapt. Over time, I developed the principles and strategies shared in *Sales God*—proven methods that worked for me and countless others.

This book is a product of not just knowledge, but real-world experiences. I've written this for everyone who's struggling with sales, for those who want to better understand how to connect with customers, and for the ones who are ready to break through the limits they've set for themselves.

For All Who Don't Know About Sales

If you've always thought that sales isn't for you—that it's only for those with "the gift of gab" or a special talent—let me tell you something: Sales is a skill anyone can learn. It's not about being pushy or convincing people to buy things they don't need. It's about understanding human behavior, solving problems, and building relationships that lead to trust and value.

Sales God is designed to give you the tools to unlock your potential. Whether you're looking to sell products, services, or even your ideas, the principles of sales remain the same. And once you understand them, there's no limit to what you can achieve.

So take this journey seriously. Apply what you've learned, stay persistent, and remember: success in sales isn't about magic—it's about mastering the craft, building confidence, and showing up every day ready to make things happen.

This is your moment to rise to the top and rule the sales world. Now go out there and make it happen!

www.ingramcontent.com/pod-product-compliance
Lightning Source LLC
Chambersburg PA
CBHW031629210526
45464CB00004B/1820